Paris Green

By

Gary Jonathan Janis

First Edition
Cover designed by Gary Jonathan Janis.

Library of Congress Cataloging-in-Publication Data is
available.

ISBN - 978-0-578-02458-5

Author's Note

Paris Green is a retrospective narrative. It speaks of an era, not too long ago, peculiar to an audience who, having dwelled therein, knows what of I tell. To another audience, younger or older, disenfranchised from that time and reality, I offer this as a remembrance of things past.

The time is the 1980s. The place is Chicago, Illinois. The specific latitude: The North Side. It is the love story of a disbelieving earthling and a hopeful fallen angel who find each other by chance of queer serendipity.

This is not a memoir, but rather, a fiction filled with autobiographical renderings.

A wonderful time. An awful time. I dedicate this work to the memory of Jimmy, Gregg, Kurt, and Jerry, dear friends who entered nirvana far too young.

The author, a native of Chicago, now lives in Las Vegas, Nevada.

Lastly, many thanks dearest Mona.

IN THE BEGINNING GOD CREATED FAIRIES AND
THEY MADE MEN

City of Night

-John Rechy-

1

∞

Strange eyes.

Those Paris green eyes have shifted away from their own reflection in the dusty mirror over the bar.

His eyes slide across the mirror like sharp steel blades soundlessly gliding on ice. Those eyes meet mine. We dance a little poisoned pas de deux on the dirty ice. These eyes stay with mine momentarily, then they return to themselves in the mirror, only to settle back into their own furtive arsenic gaze.

"I'll have another cognac," I say to Justine as I light another Salem. She's too big, is what I think about Justine, to do it right. I think this as I watch her move toward the snaking bar to order my drink. She's too large and mannish to be convincing is what I mean. If you're going to live in drag, as Justine does, you might as well look the part. A football player is what she looks like, this Justine: a giant, black football player in a dress. But Justine is a better cocktail waitress than any goddamn woman and a better cocksucker too, so I've been told.

The bar winds its way indifferently along the wall like an interminable delinquent river. Colored lights hanging over the bar give it a cheap cellophane glow. The smoke from my cigarette finds my eye in a seemingly deliberate act of revenge. Salem smoke sears my eye; my eyes fill with tears. Justine places the cognac down on the little round table before me.

"Don't cry none, hon," Justine teasingly says in her deep black faggot voice. I look up into her greasy made-up face. Her eyes look like cutouts from peacock feathers. Her mouth is all swollen lips made thicker by at least twenty applications of red lipstick. I can see the sewers in her eyes.

"Thanks," I say as I hand her the money for the drink and her tip. I put the tip in a rock glass that's already full of bills which she carries on a round cork and plastic tray.

"Just-e-e-n time, huh shuga?" Justine laughs like any black woman on any Chicago bus at the sound of her own simpleminded joke.

I say to Justine, as I sip the cognac, "Where's Sam tonight?"

"Sam's not doin' too good, hon. He's in da hosital again. Got dat new-moan-ya." She shakes her giant head; her black curls writhe like long coconut oiled snakes. Then the Medusa says, "Uh, uh, I think he ain't long for dis world, shuga."

"What hospital?" I ask.

"Saint Joseph's. Dat's all I know. He be too sick to talk an' you know doze doc-taz, dey don't tell a fuckin' thang."

Tomorrow I'll go see Sam Not Long For This World. Sam always said he was never sick a day in his life.

He was a hell of a bartender, my friend Sam. Too fucking bad is all I can say.

Arsenic Eyes has turned in his chair at the bar. He looks like a blond cherub fallen from grace, a potential exterminating angel. Our eyes meet again. I get the feeling that he's going to come over to my table, to disturb me even more than I have been already.

I snuff out the cigarette in a cracked red glass ashtray. I knock back the remaining cognac thinking that I should leave. The angel spreads his wings and floats over. In my mind I see street trash and hustlers and death.

The pale, bloodless face is before me, and it begins to speak. He's twelve years old going on fifty. He is beautiful and grotesque all at once and he says his name is Gabriel. It figures I think. I ask him to sit; what else have I to do anyway? Where do I have to go? Nowhere. That's it: there is nowhere to go.

With no conversation between us, I am hoping that it might stay that way but I am wrong. Gabriel is a hairburner, he tells me. But I have a feeling that that would be much too much for him. He smells of the streets.

I give Justine the wave and she swishes over to the table like hot greased lightning. She gyrates and swishes as only a black queen can. Justine the African Queen has a great big dollar sign in her chest instead of a heart. And it doesn't beat. Justine's dollar sign vibrates like an electric dildo powered by the methane gas of her rancid mind. If you would cut Justine open, dimes and quarters would pour out of her, and her plasma would be green and thick like split pea soup. She'd do anything for a buck, you bet.

"Sweet shuga," Justine gushes.

I feel sick. She winks at me like she thinks something's going on. She winks so loud I can hear her eyelid snap.

"What'll ya have, hon?" she questions, and with her big bloodshot eyes she shoots a look at the angel.

"Mmmm," she smacks her swollen red Cover Girl lips together and adds, "Sure wouldn't mind a little chicken for dinner myself."

He sits there like some kind of fricking Zen Buddhist staring at me. I look back up at the black drag and tell her to eat shit, which I suspect is right up her alley anyway.

Gabriel is drinking vodka gimlets, so I order him one, and I have another cognac.

I'm thinking of switching to scotch and water, but I'm not nearly drunk enough yet.

Justine's massive form spins away from us. Her cheap cologne is nauseating and just reapplied. Her feet are force fed into desperately tight high heels; twisted toes scream out the open fronts.

Gabriel tells me that he doesn't come here very often, that he doesn't care for the music, that he hates the people. Then why come at all is what I am thinking?

Because where else is there to go?

I find myself suddenly wishing I were a Lesbian: Lovely Lesbians. A Lesbian wouldn't put up with this shit.

The drinks are served by Justine with the understated agony of a saint. Saint Justine. Saint Justine of the Bedroom, is how it goes. She wishes, I can tell, that she were me, sitting and drinking with this chicken dinner. But what Saint Justine of the Bedroom doesn't realize is that this chicken dinner could be suicide. I'm sure that she is incapable of thinking thoughts of her own death. Animals cannot think thoughts about death. Animals cannot think.

Gabriel says he hates this place because he finds the people here pretentious. Even the name of it, he says, is pretentious: Force Majeure.

I tell him he has the right to believe whatever the hell he believes.

I also tell him that he is full of shit, that none of *this* could possibly pass as pretentious.

Hazy lightning skews off a small mirrored ball above the equally small dance floor. Tonight, everything seems small and devastatingly unimportant here. (Except for Sam who sticks on my brain like a bloody scab trying its best to heal). I must go see Sam tomorrow.

Two men, under the ball, move together like robotic G.I. Joe dolls guided by the repetitious music. They know the dance; one wonders if they know each other.

"Do you come here often?" Gabriel asks me as he sips his drink. His eyes become narrow slits.

Is this your place? is what he means. He seems so unimpressed with it all. So young and so unimpressed with everything. He has mirrors deep in his eyes like the mirror chips on the spinning ball above the tiny dance floor. And I can see two men dancing in his eyes, dancing on the mirror chips, and I know that they will never know each other.

"Yes," I tell him. "I do come here often." But I don't ask this of him because I have never seen him here, before tonight. But I know he's been here. I'm sure he's been everywhere. The way he holds the drink in his hand tells me this. He holds the drink in his hand with a desperate ennui. He holds himself the same.

He finally gets around to asking my name. I am tempted to tell him a lie. "Nicholas," I say hesitantly. And reaching across the small table to my pack of Salems he removes one. He puts the cigarette between his pouty lips and lights it off the candle that glows between us.

"Peace," he says just then and drags on the smoke.

Then he smiles. It's a strange mysterious smile, somewhere between hearing a secret or sharing one.

He says, this enigmatic little night bird, this disturbing fallen angel, "Salem, it means peace." His smile vanishes just as quickly as the smoke he exhales through his nostrils. How odd, I think.

I am not sure what to say to him. All I know is that I can sense some fear, some intense sobering fright that flows from him in waves like a constantly whispered threat. The air around him feels traumatized. Yet he appears cool, undaunted, and almost serene as he watches me, surrounded by this aura that he has created, hoping only to camouflage his intrinsic fragility beneath an even more fragile artifice.

"Do you live in the city?" Gabriel asks. He shifts nervously in his chair and diverts his gaze momentarily toward the dance floor.

I know what this is leading to. I know all the ins and outs of this conversation. Yet, suddenly, I feel fragmentized. Instinctively searching Gabriel's profiled face for the answers to questions that have not yet been asked, I hear the response leave my mouth, "Yes, not far from here." I feel, just then, that I have betrayed myself.

His icy peridot eyes return to mine.

"What about you?" I say in a voice stitched with apathy.

"On Dakin, behind the Sheridan El stop."

I finish my drink and get Justine to bring us another round. I'm through with this cognac. It's beginning to remind me of formaldehyde. And thinking that I have become embalmed enough, I switch to J.B. and water.

The bar has become uncomfortably crowded with men. Heat and smoke and the smell of sweat and booze mingle in a sort of mystical combination, a sort of pagan incense offered up to Priapus. The sting of old urine hits my nose. We're sitting too close to the john I think. I can taste the odor of cum in the air. It seeps through the pores of these men who are so hungrily in need, so feverishly in rut. Like dogs who care not for the bitches but only for each other, they wait, tails erect. There is a wild and morbid glint in their eyes, and they drool with silent insatiable lust. What was once insouciance is now *memento mori.*

Gabriel asks me if I dance. I do not dance. Not this sort of dance anyway.

Most of the men stand, packed on top of each other, near the bar. They all seem to cling to the bar as though their lives depend upon it.

Some of these men dance. They dance the dance that I do not do. These dancers, these terpsichoreans, they all seem to cling to the music (some to each other) as desperately as those who cling to the bar.

The faces are familiar to me, not all, but many. But familiarity breeds contempt. So they are my silent acquaintances and they shall always be my nameless friends who, I may show a sign of recognition to, with a nod of the head or a simple lift of the glass.

Saint Justine has vanished. She has been absorbed into this purgatory of human flesh as happily as a blood sucking crab louse in a big bush of filthy pubic hair. Forget the service now. That Justine is no longer interested in servicing you with drinks. She's made her bucks, now all she requires is the stink of the john and a cock in her mouth. It's her communion with God, you might say.

Gabriel tunes into my need for another drink. He can see it in my face I'm sure. And what else he sees is that I won't be bothered to push through this stinking crowd: that I am feeling claus-tro-pho-bic, misanthropic.

He eyes me like he's going to invite me to his place, like he's going to tell me that he has a bottle there, behind the El.

What else have I to do anyway? Where do I have to go? There is nowhere to go. Not until tomorrow at least.

A little suicide might not be such a bad idea. It couldn't be worse than this.

2

∞

Gabriel has to piss. He says this as we begin our escape. I say, "I need to get out of here. I'll meet you outside."

He sits there, not moving and stares into my eyes as though he wants to hear more, like he has missed something. Maybe he thinks I won't be there when he's through pissing. Maybe he wants me to follow him, to go with him to the john, to hold his prick while he pisses.

"I'll be outside," I say and reach for my windbreaker, which I discover has fallen off my chair and is lying on the sticky tile floor. We both get up from the table and I head for the door.

Cigarette smoke is thick in the air, and it gives substance to intersecting streams of light that would go unnoticed without it. The smoky light streams weave themselves effluently between each surge and beat of loud music that's being selfishly proffered by the D.J.

Two giant pulsing black boxes, mounted on the walls near the ceiling of the dance floor, give breath to this music. As I pass by them I feel the music in my chest. And it pounds savagely there like the rhythm of some alien heartbeat.

The lyrics of this music piss on my brain like my *friend* (with a name and a bottle behind the El) who is spraying up some urinal right now:

> *"I see a ship in the harbor I can and shall obey but if it wasn't for your misfortunes I'd be a heavenly person today. And I thought I was mistaken and I thought I heard you speak. Tell me how do I feel? Tell me now how should I feel? Now I stand here waiting. I thought I told you to leave me while I walked down to the beach. Tell me how does it feel when your heart grows cold?"*

I push through the crowd. It's like moving into something so corporeal that the grossness of it becomes surreal. The stink of cologne and sweat (no sweat smells the same) is all I can smell. That changes as soon as some drunken queen sticks his beet-red face into mine and asks, "Where you goin', handsome? The party's just taking off!" Booze breath. Amyl nitrate cologne. Namelessness personified. "Get lost," I scowl. I can't be bothered with this crap and I let him know it.

A hand in my crotch, on the ass. Whatever. Who gives a shit at this point. It's part of this scene. This mise-en-scene I can do without.

I swing the door open and I'm free.

Black spring. Dark sweet night. It's late April and already it feels like summer. This is the strange weather that I love.

Mercury lights on the street give Halsted a pale icy-blue radiance. The street is oddly empty for weather so comforting. After the long winter hibernation everything is usually out in droves.

The rats come out to play at night. The secret rats you see dressed up in business suits, on busses in the morning, discreetly reading their Wall Street Journal or The New York Times or sometimes the Chicago-Sun Times, heading for the Loop. Going to their attorney jobs, their banker jobs, their stockbroker jobs. Then out late at night dressed up in another kind of suit. The clone suit that they all wear, traveling in packs, heading to the bars, for their blow jobs.

An old woman, a sick street thing, suddenly springs from nowhere, as though she has emerged up out of some hidden fetid sewer. She has imbued the warm still air around me with her stench. She invades my public privacy. She disturbs me in the way that they all do. What did Christ say? *You will have the poor with you always.* There, that's it I think, as she asks me in some odd croaking English-like language for a handout. Her breath smells like vomit and whiskey. I reach into my pants pocket and pull out a moist bill. I think it's a buck, but it turns out to be a five. "Here," I say as I slip the five between two dirty truncated fingers, "have one on me."

I gaze into her listless bloated eyes. The old woman smiles up at me. I see a few rotted teeth. She cackles like a witch, nodding her head then shaking her head. "Thanks son," she drools, "and God bless ya."

A pack of secret rats push by the old woman as she hobbles away from me. One of them, a dark, severely groomed Mexican fagrat turns his brilliantined head toward her, as she goes on her way, and spits in her direction while he laughs like a Latin hyena. I catch his gold crucifix shimmer against his cafe au lait chest as he struts his stuff by me.

The secret rats enter the bar and Gabriel exits. He sees me. For a moment he appears surprised, and instantly that expression vaporizes into something nondescript, something like lassitude.

"It's a nice night," he says.

He walks next to me as we slowly walk toward Dakin Street, toward his apartment, his face forward. He speaks to me but doesn't look at me as he talks. I light a cigarette and offer him one which he doesn't take. I breathe the combination of the clean spring night air and the smoke into my lungs. It's ambrosia. I can smell rain in the air.

We pass by a store called Flashy Trash. Gabriel stops and looks into the store through its all glass front. The store is asleep. Its contents, the flashy trash that it's named for, trembles in a dim aura of nightlight fluorescence.

"I love this store," he tells me. And that's apparent from what he wears. I'm sure he'd own stock in the company if it existed and he could afford it. I wonder how he affords the clothes.

"I wish I owned this store," he breathes. Something like wonder or magic resonates in his voice as he says this. What he sees in this store has taken him away from himself. He has become, for a moment, like a child who hasn't seen it all. He has stepped into innocence, which is always there, a few drops of it no matter what, always circulating in the heart.

16

I see a ship in the harbor I can and shall obey but if it wasn't for your misfortunes I'd be a heavenly person today. The words of that song skim along the outskirts of my mind just then. *The poor you will always have with you.*

"Let's go," I say.

We continue walking, north, down Halsted Street.

"We'll go up to Grace," Gabriel says.

Not really listening to him, my mind focused on the face of the old street woman, I think he has uttered some queer religious non sequitur.

"What?" I turn to look at him while I take a drag off the Salem.

He responds, "We'll walk up to Grace Street and then over to Sheridan."

"Yes," I say.

The night sky is a silent indigo onyx umbrella. Light pollution from the city has eaten the stars. But the moon, which is cocaine white, is full and round and hangs in the sky high above us as we walk. There is a face on the moon made of dirt. And the dirty face is smiling down at us knowing our secret thoughts.

We walk down Grace Street, past the Faith Tabernacle, where a giant sign covered with pigeon shit tells that Al Smith is pastor. An enormous cross made of white plastic and neon and pigeon shit blazes above the entrance. Bible thumping Born Agains eat Jesus for breakfast there on Sundays. Then they go next door to the IHOP and eat pancakes covered with Aunt Jemima.

"Want to stop for some coffee?" Gabriel asks and looks back at the IHOP. I look back too and see lonely people sitting at booths by themselves.

"No. I don't think so," I say and wonder if Al Smith is sitting by himself somewhere reading his Bible.

The B train races across the El tracks which are just up ahead. The sound the metal train wheels make splits through the silent night cutting up the air. A bird or bat flirts with a street lamp; it's joined by a friend, and then there are two. Distant lightning flashes like amethyst crystal in the far west sky. The train has gone and there is no thunder. It is silent again except for the sound of our shoes on the cement sidewalk.

"It's going to rain," Gabriel reports as we walk under the serpentine El tracks.

Muddy pools of water in the dirt under the tracks sparkle as moonlight filtering through the track slats touches them. The moonlight embraced in the water illuminates garbage and rats and shadows of unknown things.

A car going east slowly drives by us. The old man behind the wheel gives us the look over. Beat it you old fuck, I think.

"I know, I can smell it in the air," I say, responding to Gabriel as I look away from the red Chevy.

We hit Sheridan and then go north.

"I used to live near here." I say this to Gabriel as I light another cigarette.

A couple of Puerto Rican teenage boys skulk past us. They are twins, but, they all are twins. Greased back black hair DA style. Skinny legs in tight tight black straight leg pants (always a basket). White socks. Black ballet slippers. White tee shirts under black leather jackets. Snake eyes.

This street is a slime pit, I think. There is no need for garbage cans on this street, they'd never be used.

"Where?" he asks.

"Near Wrigley Field," I say.

The laundromat I used to bring my clothes to is still here. I look in to it as we walk by. I knew a boy who used to bring his clothes there too. There was something about him that made me want to know him. He was strangely handsome; an erotic air hung about him, that's it. He had bad skin, acne or something, but he turned me on nonetheless. We started talking one day in that shitty little laundromat. His name was Greg, I think. Some strange Russian last name. His eyes were a pale silver-blue, misty, searching. He had black wavy hair which he wore sort of long, and it curled at the nape of his neck. He was into Genet, Garcia Marquez, and Henry Miller, and he always had a book with him.

His voice was boyish in a very manly way, nothing effete about him, except that he was queer of course. I wanted to suck his cock every time I saw him. Right there, even in the laundromat, as he sat on the dented yellow clothes dryer in his ripped up blue jeans with one knee exposed. But it never happened.

"I used to do my wash here," I say to Gabriel as we pass by the lightless laundromat.

"I still do," he says to me.

"I used to talk to this kid who'd do his wash there too. Seemed like we would always run into each other there. Always wanted to trick with him, but never did. One day while I was washing my clothes, the woman who ran the place asked me if I knew what had happened to him. I guess she'd see us talking. Anyway, I told her no, that I hadn't seen him for a while. Then she said she heard that he was killed by members of a gang who hate *maricones*. He was stabbed to death, she said."

Gabriel looks at me strangely, almost like he's going to laugh. But he doesn't. Then he looks away.

We hit Dakin and turn west.

The street is deserted and dark. The street lights are out. I smell sour garbage rotting in dumpsters in the alley behind a Mexican grocery store. A giant dog trots across the street sniffing at the ground like mad.

"There's where I live," Gabriel says, and points at a three flat near the end of the block. The building is black except for the light from the second story window. He says, "Oona must be home, the lights are on."

"Oona?" I say.

"She's my roommate. It's really her apartment." He says this sheepishly, almost like an apology, as though he's afraid to admit this to me.

"She saved my life," he says. I hear hope in his voice.

"She did?"

"Well, yes. But I don't want to talk about it. I'll tell you some other time, ok?"

"Sure." No problem I think.

We get to the door of the building.

Gabriel says, "Oona lives with God. God's her dog, I mean."

I suddenly want to laugh, but I hold it in and he continues, "You don't mind dogs, Nicholas?"

"No," I tell him. "But it's God I'll have trouble with."

The architecture of the building is post World War II tenement. The entranceway we enter, beyond the unlocked front door, reminds me of a miniature dilapidated mausoleum. It has the moldy stink of decay. A dim bare light bulb hangs over our heads dangling from a tarnished brass chain. The dirty white marble floor is cracked and wet and the walls are greasy yellow. The light bulb emits a toxic light that casts narcotic shadows of our bodies up to the second door inside. One mailbox in the wall is broken; its rusty door hangs open by bent hinges. I hear God barking above us as Gabriel opens the inner door.

"Oona," Gabriel says in almost a whisper, "probably has her boyfriend over."

We begin our ascension up the threadbare carpeted stairs. Wood creaks beneath us as we move. I smell the memory of Italian food.

"Is that a problem?" I question, not really caring one bit.

"No, she's cool, so's Speed. Speed's Oona's boyfriend." He tells me this as we make a turn up and around the first corner of the stairwell.

I hear the El race by again. I think about the people on the train. I wonder where they are going so early in the morning. I wonder where they have been.

"Speed's this mulatto dude," Gabriel says. "He's very beautiful, almost like a woman, but very macho. It's kind of frightening." Gabriel looks back at me. Then he turns his head forward again.

"He's an actor," he continues to inform me, "like Oona."

"She's an actress?" I am unimpressed with this.

We stop at a peeling brown door into which Gabriel inserts a key. One single silver key that he has extracted from his pants pocket.

"Yes," he says.

There is a brass letter "A" on the door and I can see that the number "2" is missing. I suddenly feel some sort of sadness creep up on me as I look at this peeling door without its number. I hear the dog sniffing at the floor behind the door.

A Doberman Pinscher with the personality of a poodle in love nuzzles Gabriel in the crotch. Then he moves to me and licks my hand like it's a lollipop.

"So this is God," I say.

I pat the dog on his slim black head and feel relieved.

"Good boy," Gabriel says, then says, "This is Nicholas."

The dog is wagging his stub of a tail and seems to find me to his liking.

The apartment is a gypsy caravan. Everything about it hits me as being mysterious in a cartoonish sort of way. It's overdone. It smells of patchouli and roses and garlic. There are beads hanging in doorways instead of doors. I'm waiting for Maria Ouspenskaya to part the beads and ask me if I want some tea. All the woodwork is painted over with white that is turning yellow from age.

I hear music coming from a back room, which apparently is at the end of a very long hallway. It sounds like Rachmaninoff. I think of Madame X and Lana Turner.

"They must be in the kitchen," Gabriel says, "Let's go see. I want you to meet them."

Oh boy. What fun, I think. Them. I must meet Them.

We start our passage down the hall. Crazy pictures on the walls hang crooked and tell me stories about Oona. One, a giant framed tarot card, really catches my eye. It's the High Priestess it reads: so Oona's a feminist I think, or just a witch.

We walk through a dimly lit dining room. There's a giant mahogany antique dining table, sitting on an old oriental carpet in the middle of the room, surrounded by six matching chairs. A white lace table runner bifurcates the table top. Heavy rose colored satin drapery has been hung deftly at the windows. Green potted palm plants stand in two corners, while an imposing glass and wood china cabinet, filled with china and an assortment of nik naks, gently glows to my left. The room is aswirl with the inspired taste of an old Jewish woman: Oona is a Jew I think.

We continue through this admixture of wall to wall bohemian interior design by way of another but shorter hallway.

The floor creaks with fatigue as we move. There is a naked translucent window, there in the hallway, dripping with moonlight. God sneaks by me brushing my hand with his wet, cold nose. His clicking toenails on the floor sound like a tap-dancing skeleton. Rachmaninoff has become Debussy.

Gabriel pushes open a swinging door that squeaks wildly announcing our entrance into the kitchen. Blued fluorescent light emanating from a large glass donut on the ceiling hits my eyes. I smell pot and tobacco and the ammonia of cat piss from a dirty litter box. Oona and

Speed look at us as we enter. They are sitting at a cluttered formica and steel kitchen table. A red candle in a Chianti bottle burns and drips next to an open bottle of Dry Sack sherry. There are some books on the table, I read one title: *The Glamour of Evil.*

They both look stoned. I feel like Henry in the movie *Eraserhead* meeting his girlfriend Mary's parents. I really need that drink, I think just then.

Gabriel says, as God sniffs the cat's ass by the screen door, "Hi, this is my friend Nicholas."

Since when are we friends, I wonder? I pull the Salem pack out of my windbreaker pocket and find it's fucking empty. My eyes catch the Surgeon General's warning that smoking by pregnant women may result in fetal injury, premature birth, and low birth weight. I crush the empty green pack and feel thankful that I'm not a pregnant woman or a fetus.

Oona cuts a look from Speed to me. Her marijuana glazed eyes attempt to sparkle, but they are just foggy black glass under pencil thin eyebrows. Her lashes are heavily mascaraed like Liza Minnelli's in *Cabaret.* She smiles. She has thin lips, like her eyebrows, and they are glossed with cherry red. Her little teeth are stained with nicotine and her lipstick has smeared them up. Her marzipan skin is peace lily white. Her hair, long and black, is cut just right and frames her face like wet silk. She's a beautiful living anorexic corpse.

Speed seems sullen, withdrawn, or just plain cool, I'm not sure. He has dark thick eyebrows that curve over sweatshirt-gray eyes. His eyes are chilling and feline. His sorrel hair is short and wavy and looks polished. There is one white curl near his forehead. It reminds me of a bleached worm. His complexion is light chocolate milk.

Gabriel is right, Speed is strangely beautiful in a very female way. He displays a facade of arch masculinity, which I find genuinely irritating.

The two of them are both dressed completely in black: *so* tired.

The cat turns around, hisses, and swipes a paw at God hitting him across his sniffing nose. The dog barks. The cat runs away. Gabriel moves to open the screen door and God leaps out onto the back porch.

Gabriel continues the introduction. Everything feels forced, unwanted. I'd like to get the fuck out of here, but I keep thinking that the booze is right around the corner.

"Nicholas," says Gabriel, "this is my roommate Oona."

She says hi and winks at me.

"And this is Speed, Oona's boyfriend."

He says hi. His toneless stare could bring a psychiatrist to tears.

"Nice to meet you," is how I respond. But I couldn't care less.

The ghetto blaster containing the classical tape comes to an end. Oona rises like a ghost from her red 50s style kitchen chair and floats over to the counter and flips the tape. It's Bossa Nova.

They think they're chic or something, these two, listening to Bossa Nova and drinking Dry Sack and smoking pot. They're caricatures is what they are. And the sad thing is, is that they think they're so cool.

Speed lights another joint.

Oona sits down again at her place at the table. She swings the hair back away from her face. Speed passes her the joint. I swear any minute she's going to say to me:

Have a hit off this reefer, baby, it's a gas.

She offers the joint to Gabriel. He puts it to his pale lips and greedily sucks up the smoke. He holds his breath and offers it to me.

What the fuck, I'm not nuts about it, but do it anyway. The smoke sears my throat. I hate the taste; now I really need that drink. Too fucking bad these two beatniks weren't blowing some toot. A little snow would be just the ticket, you can shove this pot shit.

I give the joint to Speed, exhale, the air comes out of my lungs sans smoke. Oona offers me a little dirty juice glass filled with sherry. I gratefully accept her gift and knock it back as I watch the two of them shotgun the joint. Christ, what a display I think, as the sherry and pot collide in my brain. I suddenly feel like I'm watching this scene through the gauze of a daydream. Not mine, someone else's.

Thankfully, Gabriel rescues me from impending brain damage. He says, "Let's go to my room Nicholas." And he moves to a cabinet over the sink and takes out a couple of plastic water tumblers. One blue, one lime green like his eyes.

He puts some ice from the freezer into a dented metal ice bucket that has two rings for handles.

"See you tomorrow," he says to Morticia and Gomez.

"Night," they respond in unison.

Saying nothing, I gesture goodbye with my hand, and following Gabriel back through the swinging door the odd couple return to their cozy little evening *a deux*.

3

∞

Gabriel's bedroom is a shoe box. A shoe box with a door instead of beads. I am grateful for this at least.

The room smells boyish, invitingly musty.

A long curtainless window, misted over with dirt and dust, permits cold bright light from the moon to swim into the room. I see a spider web hanging like fragile lace, there in the window, frosted by the light. The window has a pull down shade that is rolled like a scroll almost all the way up.

There's a mattress on the floor pushed back against the wall and into one corner. A disheveled moonlit pile of carelessness rests on the mattress. I see underwear, shirts, socks, pants, and a dried dog turd. God has slept here I think.

I stand in the center of this little cell, and I see the time glowing in red on a small digital clock resting on a dresser. It is almost two in the morning. I am tired. It's hitting me. And suddenly all I want to do is to flop down on that dirty mattress full of neglected laundry and come to rest there as ostentatiously as that turd. But Gabriel hands me a drink. Rosé on the rocks.

"Paul Masson," he says. Not my favorite, but so what, it's alcoholic.

He begins to clean up. It's done quickly, comically, and for just a moment I really think that the kid might be embarrassed. Suddenly the turd has vanished and the mattress seems a possibility.

Gabriel takes his shoes off and so do I. I put my windbreaker on an old leather chair near his dresser.

He moves to the dresser and lights a fat round candle off a match which is extracted from a long matchbook. The candle flickers briefly, dimly, then jumps alive with flame that gilts the room in tawny Port wine shadows. He asks me to pull down the window shade, which I do, all the way to the dirty mildewed sill.

I sit down on the mattress and lean back against the cold hard wall. The mattress feels almost like the wall.

Gabriel puts a metal ashtray on the floor by the mattress. He throws me a half-filled pack of Kools with the matchbook. "Go ahead," he invites, "I probably won't smoke 'em anyway."

Wonderful, I think! The boy has read my mind. And like some kind of genie, my wish was his command. I light a Kool with the matches. On the matchbook it says: *Come to the Californias.* The smoke ices my throat and lungs. I drink some wine.

Gabriel sits in the leather chair. He is silent. His silence is too much: quotidian and dull. Yet, I suspect that he is deeper than his silence.

"How did Oona save your life?" I ask while suppressing a yawn. I have to break the silence or I'd doze off for sure.

"It's a long story," he says.

His eyes, though frayed with fatigue, are focused on me as if I were a mandala. He rakes his hand through his thick, wavy blond hair. My eyes drift lazily to his crotch. I suddenly wonder how big he is.

Come to the Californias. I think of San Francisco and a sailboat in the bay.

"When I was three," Gabriel begins, "my mother was killed in a car accident."

I take a drag off the Kool and rearrange myself on the mattress in hope of getting comfortable. I have a feeling I'm going to suffer the long story.

"I was her only child and she didn't have a husband." He takes a slug of the wine in his glass and spreads his legs apart. He looks away from me and gazes at the candle flame on the fat round candle. "I was illegitimate, a bastard." It's a lugubrious pronouncement.

"And then, a born-again misbegotten waif." I say this with just a hint of humor in my voice.

He looks back at me coolly.

"Yes," he agrees. And he reaches down to the pack of Kools on the floor and lights one with the matches. He tosses the matches back by the ashtray.

"My mother, an only child, lived with her parents on a farm somewhere in Michigan. They were heavy duty Baptists and disowned her right away when they found out she was pregnant, so the story goes. So she took off to Detroit with a girlfriend."

"Amen," I say.

"She had me there and worked as a waitress and lived with this girlfriend. Then got killed."

"All in Detroit," I say and extinguish my immolated cigarette in the ashtray.

He blows smoke rings with perfection. The rings float toward me, then up to the ceiling, orphaned, crepuscular bubbles. I want to yawn again, and this time I do.

"More wine?" I ask.

The waif refills my glass from the jug and plops in an ice cube for good measure.

"Mother's girlfriend, the one she lived with, wanted to keep me, adopt me you see, but the court wanted to put me with my grandparents. They refused because I was of Satan you understand."

"Hail Satan," I whisper.

"So I ended up in a state-run orphanage." His voice drifting settles into silence.

My eyes are closed as he talks. The inner lids are movie screens, and on them I watch some film that has obviously been written by Jerzy Kosinski.

Heidi of the State continues, "A childless couple adopted me. I remember this like it was a dream. They took me home. They released me from that stinking institution, where every move you made was a fucking problem. Where a little boy or girl who was just a bit more than a baby was struck if they messed themselves, or whatever."

I open my eyes. My closed eyes make the room spin.

Lightning suddenly brightens the room in a galvanic flash, and thunder rumbles eerily in the not too distant distance.

30

"This man and woman became my mother and father erasing in time the memory of my real mother.

"My new parents were so wonderful to me. They gave me things that I didn't even know existed, like toys, and a pet dog, and a little swimming pool that sat in the shade of a giant Catalpa tree in our backyard."

He pauses and clears his throat then says, "And love."

"To love," I say raising my plastic goblet.

"I thought I was growing up in some sort of heaven." His voice drops off along with the ash from his cigarette. I give the ashtray a shove. It glides with a metallic peal over the floor to his feet and he puts the cigarette out.

He looks at me and says, "It's kind of hot, would you open the window please."

I say, "Sure." I move to the window to open it and continue, "I think we're in for a heavy storm, I might have to shut it soon."

The wind invades the room in a warm moist gust. The shade gets sucked back, slapping the window. I turn back to Gabriel. Sitting down again on the mattress I see that my host is out of his shirt and almost out of his pants.

"Getting comfortable?" I say as I light another Kool and swallow more wine.

He stops his strip at his very white cotton briefs.

"Yeah," he says sitting back in the decrepit leather chair. "Why don't you," he suggests in his so unconcerned voice, as though he couldn't give a shit if I did.

31

My eyes stay fixed on him. He has a surprisingly beautiful body, thin yet not skinny, but very toned without being muscular. This little angel also has, I see, a dick packed between his legs. The *shlong* of God, what else?

"Your story", I say as I begin to unbutton my shirt, "you interrupted yourself."

I'm not sure if care anything at all for his story. I sense it's a bit like masturbation; he's getting off on it.

He yawns, then begins again, his head rests back against the wall. With his eyes open he stares up at the ceiling. A flash of lightning illuminates his face.

"My new mother was very beautiful. She was older than her husband. Her name was Violet, and she had eyes like Elizabeth Taylor. Violet was from old money; her family had a number of businesses, mostly restaurants and hotels.

"My father, Sebastian, had inherited mucho bucks from his grandfather's estate. Independent wealth gave father perfect freedom, and his marriage to Violet only sealed his good fortune you see.

"Father was tall, the swimmer type you know, a Nordic blond with dark green eyes. He was incredibly handsome. People would always say, when they saw us together, how much I looked liked him. This made my parents, especially father, very happy.

"Violet, my mother, was the cool one. When I think about it now my sensation is that she resented me terribly. Because you see it was Sebastian, my father, who really wanted a child. A son that is."

Gabriel lifts his head to look at me, like he's punctuated his sentence with this gesture. His head goes back to the wall as he continues.

"Violet couldn't have children, or at least that's what she led people to believe. And so they adopted. But really this was the furthest desire from Violet's mind. She just wanted her husband; a child would, well you understand, distract his love from her."

Just then a creeping tingle spread over me as I listened to his story. There's more to this, I think, than meets the ear.

"Sebastian wanted, *needed*, just the right child of course. The boy had to resemble him. So they searched not for an infant but for an older child. And they eventually found a pretty little three year old boy who would become, in a sense, a toy for him."

"A toy?" I almost laugh at this.

Sighing heavily, the angel says, "Listen to what I'm saying."

I refill my glass with the Mr. Masson and throw in a couple of half melted ice cubes. Tossing my shirt to the end of the mattress I pull off my socks and Levis, throwing them with the shirt. I, unlike Gabriel, wear no underwear.

"Go on," I say as I move back against two rather lean pillows by the wall.

His camera eyes slowly pan over me as he introduces my nakedness to himself. Dispassionately, his peregrine eyes return to the peeling ceiling, but I see his cock stir beneath that white cotton.

The dark spring storm outside is coming to life in all its nocturnal glory. Spring storms always thrill me.

Their suburban violence simply touching the building-protected city with an elegant kiss of forensic reticence. As the cool and wet wind licked me from the half open window above, I moved to shut it.

"Mother was committed by her own nature to work in the family's business. She was obsessed with money and how to make it. I think too it was a way for her to take her mind off Sebastian. You'd understand this if you knew what my father looked like, Nicholas."

"A good catch, you might say?" I say lying back down, staring up at the lightning shot ceiling.

"So," I continue, too tired to care, only hoping really that my own voice, or maybe his, might lull me to quick sleep, "why did good old Elizabeth Taylor eyes want to take her mind off her hot young stud?"

"Because, Nicholas," I hear tension in his voice, "My father wanted something Violet couldn't ..." he sucks air between his teeth like he's going to cry "...could not give him."

I turn my head to look at Gabriel who has his hands over his eyes. Like he's afraid to see what he's seeing again.

I say, "You don't have to tell me this if ..."

"No," he blurts and his hands fall over his crotch, "I do ... I *need* to." And he opens his eyes again staring up into the strange somethingness of his past.

Suddenly I can't help but feel what must be the morbid thrill of a wake hopper. Going from funeral home to funeral home, entering each and every viewing room, playing the part of a long lost friend of the dearly departed. Looking around the room at all the living corpses, I wonder with creepy excitement who they all were to him. (*Oh, I was so sorry to hear. How sad, he was so* y-o-u-n-g. *My deepest sympathy.*)

"My father and I were," he continues, "inseparable. He took me on many incredible trips and almost all of them were without Violet. 'Your mother,' daddy would tell me, 'is too busy with her work.'"

"Hmm," I drink some wine and turn to prop my head up on my hand so that I can get a better look at the storyteller.

"As I got older, people began to mistake my father and me for brothers. You have to understand that Sebastian himself looked remarkably young for his age. It was weird but he really seemed ageless."

"A la Dorian Gray," I say.

"Sebastian was my only friend. Father ensured this by orchestrating every move we made, which was almost always together. He even demanded that I never refer to him as daddy or father but always by his name: Sebastian. You see, Nicholas, it was always Sebastian and Gabriel, never anything else."

Suddenly, I see Tennessee Williams doing somersaults in his grave and I say, "A martyr and an angel."

He fires a look at me and says, his voice clearly very hot, "Not funny, Nicholas. You couldn't possibly understand any of this, it's obvious."

I say coolly and softly, "I'm sorry. And you're wrong."

Gabriel then stands and moves toward me. He sits down next to me cross legged on the mattress. I can feel the heat of his body. His eyes are strangely vacant. He takes a sip of my wine and continues.

"When I was thirteen, Sebastian took me to Greece. It was a special trip, he told me, for my birthday.

"I was so excited.

"Greece was unbelievable, I thought.

"White.

"Hot.

"Glowing.

"Dark alluring people who gave it life.

"I was seduced by its earthy sensual promise. Have you ever been there?"

"No," I respond. I'm quite mystified all at once by Gabriel's vision.

"We moved all around Greece that summer. But we ended up staying on one of the small islands, Mikonos. The sky there was always a bright, cold, cloudless blue, as if the Greek gods had melted countless diamonds and sapphires together in a never ending canopy that stretched over the earth.

"A friend had offered father the use of his villa on the island while he was in Europe."

"Don't you mean Sebastian?"

"*Sebastian* and I, we had the villa till the end of summer. On that island, Nicholas, I learned many things that up until then I knew nothing of."

"Such as?" I ask him, this queer and provocative raconteur.

"Such as the taste of the gifts of the unspoiled earth and the sea. The taste of wine and how it feels when you drink it. And something so decidedly perfect and beautiful: the taste of a father's love that in its all consuming way had never been a father's, but a lover's."

That's it, I say to myself. And it's a let down.

"Sebastian initiated me into manhood. He said to me that summer on Mikonos, on my birthday, 'Gabriel, today you are a man.' He taught me what it was like to be with a man."

I feel strangely betrayed somehow. I knew all along what this was leading to and now, well so what? I think.

"So where's your lover now?" I ask.

At that the angel spreads his wings again but he does not fly. He embraces me, and with the sound of tears in his soft voice he whispers, as he lays his head on my chest, "He got sick, Nicholas, and died."

4

∞

I remember.

I remember sitting quietly on the large dusty sofa in my parents' living room. I knew it was dusty because whenever I slapped one of its maroon colored cushions with the palm of my hand, a cloud of smoke would rise up out of it glittering momentarily in the sunlight. Sitting there very still that day I observed through the curving bay window the tall green trees which lined the yard in front of our house. I saw quite clearly the tree leaves trembling in the rustling wind of the warm summer afternoon. I could hear the wind but what I really heard was a hiss of leaves in the breeze-touched branches of the trees. The old grandfather clock standing rigidly at attention in a shadowed corner of the room became a monotonous metronome. As each new hour arrived the tall aloof clock chimed. With every passing hour the bright square of light on the carpeted floor became smaller the light on the bay window less intense. I remember the stillness in the house. The hushed voices of my mother and grandmother framed the stillness while my own voice was imprisoned in silence. I could smell the dinner that my grandmother was preparing in the kitchen. The kitchen seemed so far away from where I sat. The food smelled good but I had no appetite. My mother had again disappeared into their bedroom. My father who rest dying on their bed had become a mystery to me. No longer was this man my strong and loving father but something alien declining in death. Although it wasn't clear to me then what death was I knew that its approach had raped our house of happiness. I remember looking at the long wooden crucifix on the wall near my parents' bedroom. A yellow bar of sunlight fell over the face of Jesus. I said a prayer to Jesus in my mind while I studied his face shining in the golden light. I asked Jesus to let my father be all right again. I said he could take me to heaven in his place. I told Jesus that it would not be a good thing for my mother to be without him. When my mother came out of the dark room I saw that her face was tear stained. She looked tired and weak and shaken. My grandmother emerged from the kitchen wiping her thin wrinkled hands on the stained blue cotton apron tied around her waist. She moved to my mother from whose lips fell unutterable broken words. They then held each other each crying into the other's shoulder. The two women soon moved to me. My mother knelt down before me taking my small hands into hers which were much larger and cold. My grandmother standing behind her continued to shudder in grief. Nicholas your father has gone to heaven my mother said softly. He is with Jesus now. And I remember that I closed my eyes but could not cry.

5

∞

The rain rushing against Gabriel's bedroom window is hypnotic to me. But the lightning and thunder, which simultaneously explodes between shorter and shorter increments of time, keeps me awake.

Occasionally I open my eyes and look around the shitty room. The candle flame, I notice, has gone out.

The angel and I lie together on his stinking little flat mattress. But I'm too tired to care how uncomfortable it is and too drunk to get a hard on.

My fingers travel in slow delicate circles down the angel's back. His skin is soft and cool and hairless. My hand reaches his ass. I let it rest there.

Gabriel holds on to me like he's found Sebastian again in Greece. What a thought! It's just because I'm blond and older than him I think. And because he's been drinking: booze can work miracles.

As I think this I let my other hand move languidly through his thick golden hair. His wavy hair is close to my face, and it smells like cigarette smoke and shampoo. Gabriel's smooth cheek rests against my chest, while his legs have become entwined with mine. His breathing has grown deeper. I'm sure he's fallen asleep.

I wonder as we lie there, as I listen to the rain and thunder and his rhythmic breathing, from what did Sebastian die, and how did Oona save his life?

Suddenly I feel myself caring.

As sleep begins to overtake me in its drifting current, I wonder too, what I have done wrong to evoke this contemptible sensation.

6

∞

Birds are singing madly in my brain. A wicked laser beam of hot white light is trespassing across my closed eyelids. The skin that I am not too tightly wrapped in, at just this moment, feels like it is crawling. And my mouth is steaming inside with an old piss sourness of last night's wine.

I open my eyes and turn my head away from the window. The window shade has been pulled up somewhat, along with the window, and the invading light that is attacking my rather less than real sense of reality is enough to make me puke. Thank God, I think, the birds are really outside.

Sitting up, I look dazedly around the room, trying to recall just whose room it is. And then it all comes back to me like a rush of butyl nitrate.

My prick is stiff with a hard-on for the john. I feel like jerking off, but I settle for a cigarette instead. Anyway, I don't know who the hell might come banging brainlessly into this room, catching me with me in hand.

I discover a note next to me on the mattress. It's a love letter from the angel.

Nicholas, thanx for last night. I really needed someone to talk to. Had to be at work early this morning, hairburning starts at the crack of dawn on Saturdays. Stay as long as you like. I put a clean towel on the chair if you want to take a shower before you go. I like you, Nicholas. I really want to see you again. Please leave me your phone number if that sounds good to you. Love, Gabriel.

"So he does work," I say out loud.

My piss erection has deflated.

I see that the Mr. Masson jug is empty. It's hangover city and it ain't very pretty. A line or two of snow would do the trick I think, but I'd settle for a couple of Valium. Up or down, either way I'm going to pay for this, until my first (or is it my next, I'm never really sure) drink.

Standing, I look at the time which is electronically manifesting itself, in glowing red numbers, on the dresser. It's almost eleven-thirty. Not bad.

I catch my reflection in a big, square, cracked mirror over the dresser. I don't recall it being there last night. But it is now, I can see, and I look like hell. The crack runs down right across my face.

"*Dominus vobiscum*," I say to the reflection.

Picking up the white towel on the chair, I wrap it around my waist. I'll take a shower, that's it. I'll take a shower, get a cup of coffee, and go see Sam at Saint Joseph's. Anyway, the hospital just might be the right place to go, considering the way I feel.

♟

Shit, showered and-- and I'm just ready to leave Gabriel's lovely hideaway, when I hear the oscine voice of Oona The Mawky Bird.

"Would you like a cup of coffee before you go?" she asks from a distance.

From the sound of things she's beyond the hall, in the dining room, sitting amidst potted palms and nik naks.

Thinking that that cup of coffee might be the thing, I tell her I would and head down the hall.

A strange bird indeed, is this Oona. My eyes, adjusting to the candle-lit dimness of the room, catch her sitting there at the head of the enormous old table. Her paste white face glows out from beneath the red rash of a silk turban that is tightly wrapped around her head. Her body is enshroud in a satin-black, pencil-thin tunic, while she sports barbaric jewelry that has obviously been designed by some no-talent friend. Just the thread of a smile crosses her blood colored lips. She is stationed there like a sibylline pussycat guarding a dying mouse. Her pale hand, heavy with rings, snakes to the silver coffee service that rests upon a tarnished tray before her.

"The coffee," says Oona in a decadent monotone as she pours, "is laced with chicory and cocaine. One lump or two?" she asks while lifting a tiny pair of silver tongs from the tray, then tapping the sugar bowl. The tongs catch and hold the light of an electric candelabrum which flickers at the center of the table.

There is nothing worse, I think, than adding sugar to one's coffee, especially if it is as well made as Oona's. I tell her I drink it black, that I find the taste of chicory particularly enjoyable, to say nothing of the bitter kiss of cocaine. I am more than overjoyed to indulge in her steaming afternoon brew!

44

She asks me to sit, which I do, in the chair next to her. I suddenly smell patchouli oil, first faint, then enough to make you faint. It's patchouli oil and garlic, is what it is. Then I realize, as Oona speaks, that it is she that smells of patchouli, and her breath that smells of garlic. How lovely!

"Did you," she is asking me, "have a nice evening with Gabriel?"

I drink the hot coffee from a chipped china cup. I look at the cup's delicate spiraling flower pattern, and I think of my grandmother, seeing her in some faraway kitchen, preparing a meal.

"Gabriel is a very nice boy," I say to her without affection. As if he means nothing to me which he does.

Oona says, as she lights a black cigarette, "Gabriel is very special to me, Nicholas. Did he tell you how we met?"

She exhales smoke from her nostrils like some kind of cabaret chanteuse. Just then I notice that she is cross eyed. The whole picture that she creates is wildly laughable. But, I am polite at times, so I suppress the giggles.

I say to her, as I feel the caffeine and cocaine do a flash dance in my brain pan, "No, not quite. Why don't you."

I'll listen. What the hell, I'm here. All I was going to do anyway was to go see Sam. And Sam's not going anywhere, that's for sure.

So she starts to talk and I listen. I smell garlic and patchouli and the pungent smoke of her black cigarette. She offers me a black cigarette, which I accept, that she lights with her green Godzilla dragon lighter.

The duenna speaks: "A long time ago, two young girls who were best friends, who were from the farm lands of Michigan, ran away to Detroit together.

"They did this because one of them, the younger of the two, was pregnant and not married. Her parents disowned her. They disowned her because to them this was a grave and unforgivable sin in the eyes of God."

"Not to mention their own," I add.

I finish the coffee, and she refills my cup as she continues talking.

"In Detroit the two girls got jobs as waitresses, and the pregnant one worked right up until she went into labor.

"She gave birth to a beautiful baby boy, who she said looked like an angel, and so she named him Gabriel."

How heartwarming, I think. *This* must be what they call deja vu, I say to myself as I sip my coffee.

"On the day that the baby was born, Gabriel's mother made her best friend promise her, that if anything happened to her, the friend would look after Gabriel as if he were her own son. It was an odd premonition, as though she could see her own devastated future on that very happy day."

Oona stares like a tranquilized clairvoyant into the fake electric fire of her sparkling candelabrum. Her voice is low. She is most definitely an actress as Gabriel had warned.

"When Gabriel was three years old," she continues, "just a little boy, his mother was killed in a car accident.

"Her friend tried to keep her promise to his mother, but the state intervened and put him in an orphanage. You

46

can imagine that her friend was crushed. Rendered powerless. But she was not defeated."

Oona pours herself more coffee. She sips it as she continues with this grim fairy tale.

"The friend never really let Gabriel out of her sight-- as best she could, that is.

"Like a spy, she found things out.

"She found out that the boy had been adopted by a young, wealthy couple from Grosse Pointe, who said that they could not have children of their own.

"The friend knew some people, you see, who could give her information."

She warms up my almost empty cup with more coffee.

"Reading the society columns in every paper, from time to time she would spot a telling piece. The stepfather was a very rich, oh how shall I say, jet-setter, of certain international repute. He was also an extremely handsome man, who had as it turns out, an extremely big appetite for beautiful young boys."

Oona eyes me like she thinks I'm going to look shocked. I hear her dog, or at least I think it's her dog, angrily barking from beyond the kitchen. I look to, and then away from the short hallway leading into the kitchen and say, "God sounds a bit hungry this afternoon."

"He's fine. He's outside on the porch. Would you like another cigarette?" she asks.

"No," I say. Her black cigarettes taste like shit and they smell worse. Then I say, "Go on with your story." My nerves are like hot electric tight ropes, but I hold up the cup for more coffee.

She begins again as she pours, "Gabriel's adoptive mother had little if anything at all to do with him. To this day, Nicholas, the woman does not recognize the boy-- in any way what-so-ever."

Oona pauses to light one of her stink sticks. She sucks up the smoke in a French inhale and continues speaking, each word floats from her tense red lips embraced in a cottony gray cocoon.

"Gabriel's stepfather raised him to become his lover, not his son. He never wanted a child; what he wanted was a legal boy lover.

"He was also a selfish and driven man, obsessed with sex. It was a slavish obsession that grew more painfully demanding as he got older. He was a vampire, really, who fed on sex with boys and young men."

This is too much I think! A vampire: *we're all vampires, Oona baby*! And I tell her I have to take a leak. But it's a piss and a shit, I just bet. Perhaps I'll puke too. I'd like to puke up my coffee-filled guts right on her red wrapped head.

⚱

The oblong bathroom is cool and dark. Mildew and soapy crud have hardened in immutable friendship between the cracks of the tiny square black and white tiles on the floor. A large cockroach runs around the sink, scurrying into a hole between the bathtub and the wet wall, it disappears.

I look down into the white toilet and see, through a pond of clear motionless water, the irremovable stains of thousands of human defecations and urinations. I have always wondered where the countless tons of human shit and countless gallons of human piss go, after they leave these infinite number of white stained bowls. Worse yet, I wonder what poor fuck is toiling away at the other end of these deep dark tunnels of love.

That's it, I say to myself as my bare ass touches the cold unyielding plastic seat of the commode. I have just remembered the graffito of a truly awakened man that I read while taking a crap once in some john: *Life is like a shit sandwich. The more bread you have the less shit you have to eat.*

⇑

"Listen, Oona," I begin as I make my arrival, again, into the dark dining room, "I really need to get going."

"But I haven't finished the story. Not that it's a story, you understand." Her voice contains a ghosty touch of urgency. It's the unfinishedness about it all that's got her, I think.

Looking into her glassy crossed eyes; hearing that flat yet full actress voice; thinking about how much shit she has had to eat; I sit next to her again and listen to the rest of her not-a-story story.

"As Gabriel got older, his stepfather grew less and less interested in him. He was definitely a hunter. And because he was very rich, with lots of connections, the entire world was his hunting ground.

"Eventually, Gabriel was completely pushed to the side. Not a son, really, and no longer a lover, Gabriel found himself, again, quite alone. Disenfranchised from a non-family."

She offers me another cup of coffee but I refuse.

"When Gabriel was twenty, his stepfather died in a hospital in France," Oona reports this like some anchorwoman on the ten o'clock news.

"What of?" I ask, but I already know.

"He died of brain cancer, Nicholas. Because of AIDS."

Come to the Californias

We are not unfamiliar with the term.

Again, a greasy nausea knots my stomach and I ask, "How did you save Gabriel's life, Oona?"

"I was Gabriel's real mother's best friend, get it? I kept my promise to her after all." She tells me this with something proclamatory gleaming in her dark eyes.

And now it makes perfect sense; she certainly could be old enough.

"Gabriel took off," she continues, "and I found out where he went. He split from the mother who wanted nothing more than to get rid of him. He tried to kill himself.

"The stepfather had a will. Gabriel was given nothing; a clause in the will stated that only flesh and blood children would be entitled to the estate, not those by adoption. All of the money and property went to the wife. This was written in cement before Gabriel was even born."

"You kept him from killing himself, is that it?"

"I traced him to some godforsaken flophouse. He was drinking very heavily, and taking pills, and--" she clears her throat, "and thank God he wasn't shooting up."

She looks straight at me then, like she can see through me, like I am transparent, nothing.

She speaks slowly, her words strung together on a string of implacable sobriety, "Nicholas, it's very, very strange, the human mind." She touches, with her long thin fingers, a weird gold locket that hangs like a noose around her neck. "Gabriel, he remembered me, after all those years." Her eyes fill with tears, one tear escapes the welling pool of one eye. "Even in his devastated emotional state, Gabriel knew who I was." She dabs her eyes with a red cloth napkin that she has picked up from the table.

"I don't know what to say," I say. But I know that I need to get the fuck out of here. Either Gabriel and this bird lady have been playing a grotesque little parlor game with last nights trick, hoping for God knows what, or it's the real thing and that's even worse.

"I'm really sorry about all that Oona, but he seems to be doing much better. He even works. Anyway I have to go see a friend in the hospital, so--"

She becomes animated, out of character almost, as she tells me that: "Gabriel needs a special friend, you understand, Nicholas. He told me, before he left this morning, that he'd like to see you again. There's something about you, you know?"

"No," I say, "I don't know."

"No, perhaps you don't." And she stands up and moves to her china cabinet. She pulls out a drawer and removes a large brown mailing envelope. She returns to her chair. She opens the envelope and extracts a newspaper clipping, then she hands it to me. "Take a look," she says.

I hold the clipping nearer to the candelabrum, to get a better look. It's a picture of a man standing between two women. It's a picture taken at some party. The man suddenly appears very familiar. This guy looks like me I think, and then comes the punch in the stomach.

"That man," Oona informs me, "was Gabriel's stepfather, Sebastian."

"It's-- uncanny," I say to her, with a drawling British twist of the voice that sounds something like Boris Karloff.

I am irreverent, I admit. This is some phenomena I should respect, but that's just it. The seriousness of the situation sends me reeling. What I want to do, am compelled to do that is, is to flush this toilet. Suddenly I feel like laughing, but I know if I do I'll end up crying, and baby I've cried enough.

Looking back into her eyes, I give her the clipping and she secrets it again inside the envelope.

"I was stoned last night, Nicholas, when Gabriel brought you in to meet me and Speed. But I knew it wasn't the pot and wine that made me see what Gabriel was seeing. It blew my mind. It blew Gabriel's mind too."

Their minds have been blown! Like fuses. Fuses screwed into the wrong fuse box. So what the fuck am I, I think? I think, that they think, that I am the electrician, come to tighten a few loose screws.

"Oona, I have to go," I say and I stand to leave.
"But--"

I am at the front door. Her "But--", has been left behind. Then I remember that I put my windbreaker on the leather chair in the angel's bedroom. It's there, right where I deposited it, this morning.

I see the note again. The love letter is there on his mattress.

I see a ship in the harbor I can and shall obey but if it wasn't for your misfortunes I'd be a heavenly person today.

There is a pen on the angel's dresser, I see. The name of the bar that we were at, last night, is imprinted on it in gold: Force Majeure.

I pick up the note, and at the bottom I write my phone number and sign my name. I put the pen on top of the note.

"Force majeure," I say to my reflection in the big, cracked mirror over the dresser.

"How very true."

7

∞

The afternoon air is sultry. The sun, bright yellow, is blazing in an aquamarine sky that is innocent of clouds. There is no wind, which is so unusual, because this *is* the windy city. Thank God I have my sunglasses.

I am sweating. I am hung over, hungry without an appetite, and I am coming down from cocaine but buzzing from caffeine. There is a jackhammer inside my skull hammering away at my brain. I am walking to see a dying friend. I think I need a drink.

A cold beer and a shot of J.D. would be just the ticket, so I stop in at Force Majeure and sit down at the bar. The place is empty except for Gary, the bartender. It is cool and dark inside, and the stink of old booze makes my mouth water. Gary comes to my rescue just in the nick of time. I take off the Ray Bans and lay them on the bar next to an ashtray.

Gary, the cowboy, owns the place. He looks like a bronco buster at the rodeo. He's a southern fag from Texas, and from the look of what he carries in his Levis, he's about as big.

Gary smokes Marlboros (of course) but *she* likes them with menthol. I ask him for one as he pours the beer and shot."Sure thing, Nick." And he throws me the pack. I take two.

The cowboy has almost lost his southern drawl; all that remains is a hint of mint julep. Chicago has a way of doing that to you. Even the blacks sound different here. But then that should come as no surprise, because they sound different anywhere.

I once met this black dancer at the baths. His name was David. He was a beautiful, muscular, black adonis. I sucked his cock in the steam room while clouds of steam were belched up around us. His skin was hot wet licorice, and I trailed my tongue up his stomach to his chest. I sucked at his neck and then his mouth. And I'll always remember how he sounded when he told me his name and asked for mine. He spoke with perfect unadulterated English. How refreshing, I thought.

Gary asks me what's going on? I tell him that I'm on my way to see Sam. I knock back the Jack Daniels and chase it with a mouthful of beer. Christ never tasted this good! I light a Marlboro and take a heavy drag. I'm starting to feel like myself again.

"Sam's doin' better," Gary tells me. "They thought they were goin' to lose him, but his turn for the worse, turned for the good. He can breathe now without the oxygen mask," he says, "and they took him off the morphine. The AZT isn't helpin' like they hoped."

"Nick," Gary adds, "Sam's got K.S."

"Jesus Fucking Christ!" I want to throw the shot glass against the wall, but I slide it to the cowboy for a refill instead.

"Take it easy," Gary tells me. "Gettin' upset's not gonna do any good, Nick."

He puts the shot down on the bar in front of me.

I take a drag off the cigarette. I shoot the shot down my throat; the beer goes with it real smooth and cold.

My mind suddenly feels lighter, and I remember how much Sam liked his boilermakers. That's what he called them: boilermakers, a shot and a beer. Shit, Sam could drink any fucking body under the bar. That Sam could almost out drink me.

I finish the beer and give Gary the high sign for another.

He takes the mug and puts it under the tap; his giant hairy hand encircles the tap handle, and he gives it a pull. I remember the night I went home with the cowboy. I can still feel that hand around my prick when I think about it.

"You better take it easy, Nick, if you're goin' to the hospital." Gary speaks his mind. He doesn't drink. Says he never did.

I tell him he's full of shit, that he knows I can hold the booze better than anyone.

He says, "Ah know, Nick." His I-s always sound like Ah-s. And then he says, "But why do you have to drink so darn much?"

What a riot I think! This bastard makes a fortune selling the fucking stuff, and he asks me *why* I drink it.

He deserves an answer I suppose. He is my friend, so I tell him, "Gary, it's like what this old drag queen once said to me, one night, while we were both getting liquored up in some joint over on Clark street. I asked her the same stupid question and she said: 'D-a-h-l-i-n-g, the reason *why* I drink so much, is

56

because it gives me something to do while I'm waiting to get drunk.'" I say it like Tallulah Bankhead, but I wave the cigarette in the air like Davis. I tap the shot glass on the bar. One more won't hurt; it can only help.

Gary shakes his head and laughs as he picks up the glass. A little camp to sooth the savage breast. It's the thing, you see.

Just then, Justine swims into the bar. What a sight!

"Speaking of the devil," Gary's baritone voice proclaims.

Shit, shuga, who be speakin' about da devil?" Justine gushes in fake fright as she screws her mammoth self into the bar chair next to me. Her face is all teeth.

"It's the wrong devil," I say to Gary, but I am looking at Justine.

Justine is sweaty, and she smells like it. She smells like gardenias and b.o. And she is all out of breath, this big beefy drag queen. She's huffing and puffing like she's been chased by the law, which is probably a safe bet. Maybe she'll have a heart attack; she says she's had one before. Which is why she can't have the *operation*. She says, "It wou' be too hard on ma po old heart."

"Where's all da trade?" Justine asks as she scans the empty bar.

To Justine the trade, as she so demurely puts it, is her cocktail customers.

Gary says, "You know it's too early, Just. Anyway, what the hell are you doing here?"

He calls her Just. Or sometimes he calls her Just-In-Time, because she's either late or just in time to start her shift, which is why I'm shocked as shit to see her now. Maybe she had a stroke; she doesn't know what time it is.

"Ah shuga," Justine laughs right in my face. She's been eating onions.

"Just stopped by, on her way to da sto, to ax how Sam be doin'?" She shakes her head and says, "Ya knows dey took ma phone out."

They took out her phone because she used the party lines so much she gave herself a bill of over a grand. The *po* fuck, is all I can say. They should have let her keep the goddamn phone; they should have paid the fucking bill for her. The party lines kept her out of the bookstores and the alleys at least.

"Sam's better," Gary says.

"Po, Sam." Justine's already glazed cesspit eyes fill with tears. She picks up a wet bar napkin and dabs at them. The napkin's now covered with greasy blue mascara.

"I'd like ta go ova dare to dat hosital, buf ya know hun, I scared to def of dem places."

"I'll drink to that," I say to Justine and ask her if I can buy her one: "For courage," I encourage.

She thanks me so much but declines my most generous offer. How can that be I think? She's always ready for a free one.

So I'm through with this drinking, until later that is. After a piss in Gary's foul crapper I'm on my way. And I tell Justine and then Gary that I'll give Sam their love.

8

∞

Saint Joseph's Hospital stands at the corners of Sheridan, Diversey, and Lake Shore Drive. The giant structure overlooks The Lake and Lincoln Park. The Zoo is not far.

There is a statue in the park, just across Diversey. It is a giant man on whose knee is perched a giant bird. Over the years a patina of green has insinuated itself upon the statue. The inscription at the bottom reads: To Goethe – The Mastermind of the German People. There is a street in Chicago called Goethe; almost no one says it correctly, especially the bus drivers. Funny, you would think that because it's called Lincoln Park there would be a statue of Abraham; instead we have Goethe The Master Mind.

I notice as I walk down Sheridan, past Surf Street, that the trees are starting to bud. It's too early I think; it could still snow, and probably will, knowing how I know Chicago.

People in Chicago, too, are like its weather: unpredictably cold, hot, windy. I have lived in many places; I have been around, and I have never seen a people, quite like the people, that live in Chicago. It's a nice place to live, but I wouldn't want to visit here.

As I walk down the bright white hospital corridor, next to a few free-floating nuns, and pass the little pastel gift shop, I think that I should buy Sam a plant, maybe some flowers. But then I remember someone, a doctor I think, saying to me once, that that might not be such a good idea. He said, 'In the case of AIDS, the patient is so susceptible to infectious agents, even plants and flowers given as gifts might present a problem.'

I wondered if what he said was true, and how terribly sad if it were. I decide to skip the plant. I'll ask Sam what he needs, which is a much better idea I think.

Sam is alone in his room. The other bed is deserted. I walk slowly into the silent room, my heart is beating quickly. The room is warm and dark, but a bit of sunlight seeps into it, like watery chicken bullion through the nearly closed beige curtains.

Sam is sleeping.

I quietly sit down in the chair next to his bed. The room smells of chemicals. I think of a dark room like this, with smells like this, that I once used to visit. It seems so long ago.

There are no plants or flowers in this room, though there are many cards from many friends. The cards are standing on a table next to Sam. Their faces look in his direction, but these faces all tell lies. One says: *Get well soon.* Another: *Hurry up and get better, we miss you!*

They don't make cards for AIDS patients, I say to myself, as I look over this assortment of attempted good intention. Anyway, what would these cards say if they did? How would Hallmark tell it? Like it is. I got a card on my twenty-eighth birthday. There was a photo on the front of this card, of some queen dressed up like Joan Crawford. She was in repose in a red silk-lined coffin, holding up the lid. The card said inside: *On your birthday wake up and live, because being dead is such a drag!* They could always replace the word birthday with the word deathbed. Maybe that's what these cards would say.

Sam is covered up with a blanket. His face is gray; he has dark circles around sunken eyes. There's a purple blotch growling on his right cheek. He looks skullish.

A tall steel stand, suspending several clear plastic bags of fluid, is standing guard over him. From these bags, these mysterious liquids enter Sam's body through long clear plastic tubes which terminate at his arms. A clear tube bringing him oxygen snakes up into his nose from some unseen source.

On this bed, before me, is what once used to be a beautiful, strong, healthy man. And Sam would say: *I've never been sick a day in my life, Nick.*

"Too fucking bad," I whisper.

Sam opens his eyes. His eyes float like ghosts in my direction. He tries to smile. His lips are white and cracked. The smile fluttering, fades.

"Sammy," I say, leaning forward. I lightly squeeze his arm through the blanket.

"Nicky--" he wheezes, coughs, "how's this for kicks?"

"I hear you're doing better, kiddo." I try to smile but it's so fucking hard. What's worse is keeping the tears out of the eyes.

Pain, I've seen this face before.

"Yeah," he whispers and turns his head toward me, "now I'm a regular morphine addict too."

He tries to laugh but his attempt turns into a spasm of choking. He's shivering now and it's so warm in here. Jesus Christ, what the fuck?

"Can I get you something, Sam?"

His shivers stop momentarily, then they start again.

"Water," he says through chattering teeth.

I look around his area and spot a blue plastic carafe next to a blue plastic cup. I move to get them. I pour the water into the cup and offer it to Sam, holding his head with my free hand for support.

"Here's your boilermaker, buddy," I say.

It's very difficult for Sam to drink. Most of the water ends up running down his face. I get a towel and wipe him up.

"So, Sammy, how they been treating you in here?"

"It's not home, Nick," he wheezes, "but it'll do."

He closes his eyes then whispers: "All this for a little dirty anonymous sex."

My eyes catch the figure of a risen Jesus on the cross above Sam's bed. I close my eyes too.

Come to the Californias

The name of our sailboat was Hollywood Mary. David and I named it that, after my Aunt Mary, because that was her moniker even though she lived in Chicago.

62

Hollywood Mary was the Toddlin' Town's darling of the Depression Era. A real party girl, that Mary; she could out drink the best of them.

Aunt Mary had an itch that needed scratching, but it never was, really.

Hollywood Mary was the mistress of some rich old man named Hanley, Whitney Hanley, or something like that. He gave her furs, jewelry, and a long gleaming white sedan that came equipped with gasoline tickets. *Gasoline tickets*: it was the Depression.

Mary's thing was fast cars and even faster men. She had a piston driven ass, and spit-fire mouth, either of which I have been told could keep any of those men in their place.

Eventually she married a crime reporter who worked at one of the big Chicago papers. O'Malley was his name. That lasted about a month; Hollywood Mary was not the settling kind.

Aunt Mary died one hot August evening; the year was nineteen seventy. She died in her sleep, alone in her bed in a rundown house in Bridgeport, Illinois, her little black and white t.v. tuned into the Honeymooners. The furs and jewelry, and her gleaming white sedan were long gone. She was sixty years old. And that's what comes from too much pills and liquor, so the song goes.

David loved that boat, and when we had to sell it to help pay for his medical bills, he almost died that day. Considering how he suffered until he did, that might not have been such a bad idea.

David's doctor told him that he had AIDS when an infection in his ear would not get better.

David begged me to get tested: "To be on the safe side, Nick," he said.

But I said what the fuck? What difference does it make now? "There is no safe side, David."

I went to David's doctor for the tests-- to please David. I knew what the results were going to be before I went for those tests. But I was wrong. All were negative.

Christ, how can that be I screamed inside? If David has it, then as sure as the devil's in hell, I have to have it too. I tested once more, before I moved to Chicago, shortly after David had died. Negative again. Miracle O' Miracles.

I screamed again, but this time my scream was of smothering guilt, rage, hostility.

David, my one and only, this significant other, my *lover* of seven years, was dead. He died from some purple cancer from another planet that had devoured him. I held him in my arms while he died. He weighed eighty pounds reduced from one hundred and eighty. And he was only thirty-five years old when his kidneys finally gave out and his heart stopped beating.

I left San Francisco soon after that. I moved back to Chicago, far away from this horrible, unforgivable *thing* that had happened.

David was cremated two days after he died. I remember that it was harder than hell to get an undertaker to touch him. *Him.* Not his corpse, not his dead body. He was still *him* to me, still David, whom I loved so very much.

My being, whatever the fuck that means, was cremated along with him that spring day. It was a day very much like today, as I sit here with Sam in this dark, warm hospital room, watching him die, just like David.

Sam is sleeping. His breathing is labored and arrhythmic. It's time to go I think.

I stand to leave, but before I leave I am compelled to kiss Sam. I have a feeling it won't be long now. So I silently move over him and bend down to touch his mouth with mine.

His lips are cold.

Gently wiping the hair back off his forehead, I whisper at his ear, "Sam, I love you. So does Gary and so does Justine."

9

∞

Walking west down Diversey, toward Pine Grove, my stomach has suddenly screamed to life. It is leading me to its favorite haunt, Gaitano's Bistro.

I look at my watch and see that five o'clock will be quick to have me in its grips; soon it will be nine, then midnight, then Sunday.

That's how time flies I think, and it's shit.

"Are you familiar with Nam-myoho-renge-kyo?" asks this woman as I approach her and her female companion. They look like a couple of dykes these two, a couple of white dykes blabbering Japanese. The fat one, exploding out of her ice-washed jeans, the one who hasn't questioned me about my familiarity, is attempting to stick a yellow pamphlet up my nose. I suspect it contains their sentimental oriental philosophy.

I say to them, "Does it cure AIDS?"

The not so fat one, her bewildered milky blue eyes, two great gross interlocking circles of concern begging for my conversion, says to me: "It cures anything if you chant it devotedly."

Chant it devotedly! What a joke I think. I'd like to slap her right across her bony face. I want to kick the baby elephant up her fat ass. But instead, I am gracious. I tell them that they should take it to Dr. C. Everett Koop, that they have most certainly unearthed a miracle, to say nothing of the immediate bankruptcy of Burroughs Wellcome.

I toss their piece of yellow propaganda in the nearest garbage can where it belongs.

Now I'm really starving. All I can think of is a bottle of dry red wine accompanied by Gaitano's specialty, Lasagna Florentine.

It's the best. And so is their garlic bread a la sesame seeds. I am dying just thinking about it.

The little bistro is owned by these two old queens from the Bronx, who have been married since Socrates took the poison. They even look like each other: overweight, which isn't surprising by the way they cook, balding, graying, nellie.

Gaitano's is a dark and quiet venue, very art deco, set up to provide a sense of privacy whilst grazing with the public.

There is usually an eternal wait; all the fags in town, and every other trendy straight couple want to eat here. But Ned and Tobias Gaitano, my two old campy friends, the owners, just love me: *Oh, Nicholas, we just love you, doll!* So I never have a problem getting seated at my favorite booth right away. Now how's that for it's not *what* you know?

It is still early spring, so as I leave Gaitano's I see that the sun has set. The temperature has dropped suddenly; its new wintry personality demands that I don the windbreaker, which only a few hours ago, I simply carried in my hand.

I am stuffed like a Lithuanian sausage in a very tight intestine casing. The food tonight was better than ever. And I am just precisely, just deliciously drunk.

The street lights are coming on, each one slowly burning up into singular globed flares of bright white light.

The air is crisp and cold and still. I can see my breath like steam as I walk.

The once purple sky has gone black and is dotted by a sprinkling of tiny sparkling stars that seem so very far away.

I look upward into the obsidian vault of heaven and I think of David. One of the larger stars winks at me. "David," I whisper to the star, "I hope you're happy."

Turning north I walk down Broadway. This street used to be Queer Heaven. It was the jugular vein of New Town, a main artery leading to some of the best gay bars in the city. The jugular, long since severed; Halsted street has taken its place, but without the finesse for sure.

The younger Halsted street kids today don't know what they've missed, here on this street. I think this, as I slowly walk down old run down Broadway (even a McDonald's closed up, up near Belmont!).

Years ago David and I would come to Chicago in the summers and visit friends, mostly his. The days and nights seemed to weld themselves together becoming one giant, timeless party. No one cared because no one had to.

There was no fear.

There was only desire.

The worst thing you had to think about was getting syphilis or the clap. And that you could almost always easily get rid of.

I remember, in the summers, in Chicago, a sort of bus would stop at several bars each night on the weekend. We called it the V.D. Van. It was sponsored by a gay men's health center.

A truly fabulous drag queen named Dr. Gayle Warnings was the Van's P.R. person. Dressed as a female doctor, who was made up like some kind of hooker, she would try to round up as many guys as possible for a blood test for syphilis.

I can still picture David and me, fucked up of course, on booze and poppers, and probably coke, getting into this bright white van and being tested for syphilis. What a riot! because we never tricked out on each other. At least that's what I thought.

David hated needles. I remember how he almost fainted that one time, coming out of the van, and how we had to carry him back into the bar, to throw cold water on him in the bathroom. Poor kid, I thought; what's a little blood work among friends?

Many people populate the street tonight, some going in and out of stores, others into bars and restaurants. Rheumy eyed urchins pepper the scene here and there trying their best to hustle a few bucks. A black cat grins at me as I walk by him. He's a short little fuck with a mouthful of big yellow teeth, and his jheri curl is dripping down around his neck. He's holding, in his skinny palm pink hands, a long gold chain. His cloudy black eyes say to me: 'Buy dis, ofay.' The chain is lusterless, dulled no doubt by the coconut oil that has rubbed off his hair and onto his crooked fingers. The chain instantly reminds me of almost all the windows of the busses and El trains in Chicago. Greased up windows that drip with that crap that they wear in their hair. There should be some law I think, as I look at that pathetic chain, in this shitty little creep's hands. A law like not spitting, or smoking, or playing your ghetto blaster on *da public t-r-a-n-z-p-o-t-a-s-h-o-n*. On that very same sign the law would proclaim: WEAR A SHOWER CAP ABOARD BUS MOTHER FUCKER AND NO CHAIN SELLING ALLOWED.

These are the nameless numbers that haunt this street-- all potential thieves, murderers, or just friends.

I am walking by a bar called Out Of The Closet. I know the old dyke who owns the place, and I see through the large front window that she is sitting at the bar holding court.

She is as butch as they come, a real diesel dyke this one. Her name is Josephine, but you better call her Joe if you know what's good for you.

Joe likes her girls very fem and very young, and if she were a man (something of which I'm not sure she isn't) she'd be an A #1 Card Carrying Chicken Queen, for sure.

Joe drinks shots of Jagermeister with her Budweiser in a can; never a glass for this butch lass. She's a Bud Man and a Cubs Fan, who dies for the summers so that she can live half her life at Wrigley Field. The other half she lives at her bar, taking care of business, and eating pussy.

I decide to go in. What the hell, it's too early to go home I think. I'll go in and buy Joe a shot and a beer, and she'll buy the house a few rounds (she's always good for that).

Elan is Joe's evening bartender. I see Elan joking with some good looking young black guy, who is sitting by himself at the bar, near Joe.

Elan is a beautiful transsexual who once was a beautiful boy. Joe showed me pictures once of Elan before she made the change. Elan is Greek, very dark and smoldering this one is. She's also very smart. She's working on her MBA at Northwestern. What a riot I think, as I catch her coal eyes with mine. Her Hellenic eyes sparkle like diamonds, diamonds secreted in coal. She waves at me and an enormous smile illuminates her already glowing face. You could never guess about Elan. I wonder if her boyfriend even knows?

Joe and the black guy turn to look at me as I walk over to the bar where they sit. There are a few people at the bar. Some, in groups, sit at tables near the small dance floor in the back of the room. A lesbian couple is dancing. The room is full of gray-yellow cigarette smoke, and the tape that Elan is playing over the bar's stereo system is not as loud as usual. Thank God, I say to myself.

"Well!" Joe bellows, her voice stentorianly volcanic, "It's our long lost Nicholas." She slaps her giant hand against the top of the bar and ejaculates a baronial laugh.

"Mister Joe," I say as I light a cigarette and take a seat next to her, "how's it going?"

Elan tangos over to where I have perched and says hi.

I say hi and taking her small hand in mine I give it a quick gentlemanly kiss. Her hands, I see, are professionally French manicured. Very chic I think. She laughs and follows Joe's instructions in getting me what I want to drink. J.B. on the rocks, what else?

"Everything's just great, Nick," Joe says, then asks, "How 'bout you?"

"Can't complain, Joe," I say, and notice that the black guy, sitting down the bar from me, is giving me the look over.

Joe lights a Camel (unfiltered of course) as Elan puts the drink down on the bar before me.

"Another Bud, Elan," Joe says and she swivels her chair in my direction.

She says, her face is the granite out of which seriousness is carved, "I hear Sam from the Force is pretty sick, you know him pretty well, don't you Nick?"

I take a slug of the scotch. Then I take another. "Yeah, Joe. Sam's not doing very well. As a matter of fact, I went to see him at Saint Joseph's this afternoon. He looks very bad."

"Jesus Christ," Joe sighs and shakes her head of closely cropped gray hair.

Elan deposits Joe's Bud before her with a tiny goblet of Jagermeister. On the goblet there is a stag with tremendous treelike antlers. Floating between the antlers is a crucifix. How strange I think, as I look at the little goblet. Joe lifts the can for a toast and I lift my glass. She says, "Here's to Sam."

"To Sam," I repeat, and we touch can to glass.

She drinks deeply from her little red and white aluminum well. Then she knocks back the liquor in one swallow. I take another hit of the J.B. Elan asks, "Sam's not doing well, huh, Nick?" She has overheard. Her eyes seem to have lost their diamond chips as she asks me this.

"No, he's not, Elan."

"Poor Sam," she says, as she pours a glass of white wine. She walks to the other end of the bar with the glass.

Poor Sam, I think: Poor Sam: Poor Sam: Poor Sam! I'm sick of it. I am sick to death of Poor Sam: Poor Jimmy: Poor Gregg: Poor Kurt: Poor David!

Maybe they're not as poor as we think. Just maybe they are better off than all of us poor assholes who keep saying Poor Them. Just maybe.

My cigarette, I see, has become a filter in the ashtray. I light another.

More people come into the bar. The music has grown louder.

A pretty young girl with short red hair, who couldn't be more than eighteen, is next to Joe now. Her arm is around Joe's neck, and Joe's hand is on the girl's ass. The girl is wearing a silky pink blouse that is unbuttoned down to the middle of her chest. She is braless, I notice. She looks like a very pretty boy with tits.

Joe turns to me again and says, "Nick, meet Arlene. Arlene, meet Nick. Arlene's my new girlfriend."

With that, Joe affectionately slaps Arlene's blue jean covered ass and bellows a laugh. She says, "Right, honey." But it is not a question. It's a pronouncement with only one answer that the red-haired girl gives by shaking her pretty little face in the affirmative. The denouement to this short story will be the same as always for Joe. That is, next time, Joe will introduce me to another pretty young Sapphite.

I nod to Arlene. Arlene smiles back. Her teeth are a perfect picket fence of white ivory.

The black guy has ordered another drink from Elan. The drink is placed down on the bar before him. He catches me looking at him, and he winks at me with a smile. He gets up from his chair and cuts across the floor, across the smoky dance floor, to the place where the johns are. I think about his cock as he pulls it out of his pants to take his piss. I wonder what it would be like to suck that cock.

Joe is kissing Arlene. I can't imagine them together. But then, that's my problem I think.

The music here is growing tiresome. I finish the J.B. Elan puts another down before me. It's like magic!

The black guy has returned. He sits down again and picks up his drink. But before it reaches his lips he toasts me then sips it.

Joe turns to me and says with an apologetic tone in her big bear-hug of a voice, "It was great to see you again Nick, don't be such a stranger alright? Me and Arlene gotta be goin' . "

I smile at Arlene. Arlene smiles back.

Then Joe lumbers out of her bar stool like some kind of mechanic at a demolition derby off to fix a betraying car engine.

The two love birds, holding hands, move toward the back of the bar, probably to Joe's office.

I swill down the booze in my glass and take one more drag off my cigarette, then put it out. I put a couple of bucks on the bar for Elan. It's time to leave I think.

I look back again at the black guy; he is looking at me. I wave goodnight to Elan and head for the door.

The song that's playing, as I leave, is something by Heaven Seventeen. Some song that David and I loved to dance to I remember. Funny, I think, as I hit the door, I can't remember the song's name anymore. What difference does it make anyway?

10

∞

A tremendous breath of wind blowing down from the north infused the purple night with a bluish snowy dandruff.

The pale shimmering flakes of crystallized water, illuminated by the mercury street lamps, scattered chaotically in the air as the wicked winterish wind befouled the too soon spring respite.

Walking home, Nicholas adjusted the collar of his windbreaker to shield the back of his neck from the wind's harsh attack.

Up and down the street, people scurried to their destinations, hoping to arrive wherever they were going as quickly as possible.

The falling snow, cascading in blustery waves, was being shed from gathering gray clouds that obfuscated the full moon which hung like a platinum coin in the sky.

From time to time the cold shy moon brazenly peaked through the cloudy veil, its fleeting defused rays softly touched the earth with candid apathy, heavenly indifference.

Nicholas stopped at the intersecting corners of two streets which were patrolled by traffic lights.

A stream of cars with blazing headlights traveled slowly before him, bisecting the crossing streets, temporarily closing his path.

As Nicholas waited for the traffic lights to turn green, he removed a cigarette from the half-full pack in his windbreaker pocket, and put it to his lips. Searching the windbreaker pockets for matches, he discovered that he had none.

A kind dark hand cupped by another suddenly brought flame up to the tip of the unlit cigarette that Nicholas held between his lips.

Nicholas's hands, pale by comparison, moved over the dark offering hands, guiding the flame to its destination.

The young black man closed the top of his gold lighter, extinguishing the little fire that Nicholas felt on his face.

Nicholas drew in, then exhaled the mentholated smoke, which only tasted sharper in the icy air.

At once, Nicholas recognized the man's face as his eyes came upon it. His face was the same he had seen in the bar moments ago.

The young man had, Nicholas realized just then, followed him.

"My name's Keith," he said to Nicholas, his voice soft with a hushed sensuality. He held out his cream-in-coffee colored hand.

"I'm Nicholas," Nicholas rejoined taking Keith's hand into his own.

Deliberately Nicholas searched Keith's eyes: for conspiracy, for contempt, for danger, for all the hidden things that can transmute daydreams into nightmares. But Nicholas found only gentle, dark amber eyes, untouched by those things which Nicholas held as untouchable. And there seemed to be, to Nicholas, glowing in those eyes, a serene fearless wisdom that bespoke of confidence and comfort.

The chilling night was turning colder. Each freezing breath of wind made the falling snow whip in furious gusty waves. Trees and buildings, the streets and sidewalks, and the tops of sleeping cars were becoming heavily dusted by the shimmering white powder.

"The snow seems to be sticking," Keith said looking around him.

"Yeah, and it's getting colder," said Nicholas, and then, "and you only have a sweater."

A moment, very quickly passing, separated what Nicholas had to say, from that about which he wanted to think.

There isn't time to think about some things. Then too, not all things can be thought about, regardless of time.

Sometimes there is just the irresistible force, the thing that happens without will or thought: the Act of the Gods.

"Would you like to come over to my place? It's not far," Nicholas asked, knowingly anticipating the answer.

"Sure," accepted Keith, "that would be great."

Then Keith smiled at Nicholas, his beautiful sculpted face lighting up, thrilling Nicholas in a way that he had almost forgotten.

By the time Nicholas and Keith arrived at Nicholas's apartment, they were both desperately chilled, frosted wet.

The spacious third floor loft greeted them graciously with radiating warmth and gentle light which had already automatically turned on.

The place was very modern, Keith saw, as he removed his damp shoes in the kitchen entryway; renovated chic, clean, precise, with an unfinished elegance that was divorced from anything at all that came close to antique.

This was Nicholas's style, the young man observed, as he slipped off the cold and wet sweater, handing it to his obliging host. It was his style as well he thought.

Upon their arrival home, Nicholas was compelled by desire to make his guest feel comfortable and welcome, to spend the night, as he knew Keith would, would be a pleasure unexpected and one far too long overdue.

Nicholas moved to Keith. He held in his hands an offering of cognac in crystal. The dark liquid captured within the two snifters, touched by the overhead lights, sparkled goldly in each glass like good clear coffee.

Smiling warmly, Nicholas handed Keith a glass. "To tonight," Nicholas said softly.

"To us," Keith replied.

Touching glasses they raised each to their lips and drank. Liquid light from each glass bathed the chill which permeated them with a warmth that spread magically.

Nicholas then said, "I'm going to light a fire. Why don't you get out of--" and he smiled laughing lightly, pointing to Keith's chest then to his legs, "those things. There's a nice robe in the bathroom over there." And he gestured with his hand toward the darkness, beyond the kitchen.

"That sounds like a good idea," Keith said and winked at Nicholas.

Moving with glass in hand, Keith disappeared into the shadows.

Finding the bathroom at the end of a short hallway, he entered. Flipping the switch on the wall near the door, the room appeared brightly in white light; the long blue silk robe hung invitingly on a hook near the shower. Keith placed the snifter down onto the sink's marble counter top and closed the door behind him.

Suddenly, then, Keith felt a twinge of regret, a sharp instant of discomfort, that he had come here at all. Because he knew very well, that what he saw, in both Nicholas and Nicholas's home, was what he was seeking for himself. He also knew that very soon he would be at O'Hare Airport. Later the next day he would board a jet which would speed him back home: to work, to school, to the great spider's web of ever woven responsibility that kept him captive there.

On his way back to Los Angles Keith would think about this night. And Nicholas, then a happy memory, would sadly fade just a little. With time Keith knew this memory would continue to fade like an aging sepia photograph.

Keith thought to himself then, how sad that will be, that this unexpected and wonderful encounter, would soon be nothing more than nothing at all.

Banishing these thoughts as best he could from his mind, Keith began to strip, letting his clothes fall haphazardly down to the green marble floor.

Keith looked carefully at his naked reflection that glowed superbly in the long oblong mirror on the wall over the sink.

He was proud of his athlete's body; he knew that his toned, muscled physique was a turn on.

He took another sip of cognac as he stared at himself. Turning, he reached for the blue silk robe, then draped the robe over himself. The robe was meant for a taller more broad-shouldered man. Nicholas, he thought.

Folding his clothes in a neat pile, Keith placed them on the sink's counter top. Picking up the snifter, he then deserted the room, permitting it again to return to the dark.

⚑

Nicholas regarded Keith with the provoked eyes of one who has been suddenly seduced. Seduction, as seduction goes, always being against the will, is a violation. But violation is not always a crime against the heart. It can be, just sometimes, a purifying prefigurment: a fiery arrow shot swiftly toward the comatose soul from a heavenly bow.

Nicholas was thrown off. He was beside himself. This young man who had accompanied him home made him *feel* again.

Three years had gone by since David had died. And this fierce abandonment, the terrible psychic drought that followed David's death (though Nicholas could think of it only as murder) had left him emotionally impotent, yet desperately starving, but without appetite.

Tonight, very unexpectedly, the drought ended. Abandoned hope, like water long gone in a mysterious dried up fountain, again began to flow.

⬆

Nicholas, draped with a white robe, stood near the warm glowing fireplace, arms akimbo.

The fire he had created there filled the room with trembling light. The fire light lambently painted the room's contents with hues of saffron, crimson, and copper, while fragrant pine logs burned slowly, hissing now and then, their smoke sweet like a Yule incense.

Nicholas stoked the logs with a long pointed, blackened spear.

Keith, who had silently entered the room, placed the almost empty snifter on a sofa table. Stopping to admire an oil painting that hung on the wall near to him, he seemed transfixed.

Turning, Nicholas observed Keith standing there. Leaning against the spear, holding it tightly in his hand, Nicholas felt its point pierce the oak wood floor.

"This is beautiful," Keith proclaimed, his back toward Nicholas.

"Ganymede and Zeus," offered Nicholas in a voice just above a whisper. "It's an original. Probably worth something," he finished.

Permitting the brass spear to rest again against the soapstone wall of the fire place, Nicholas moved toward a tall mahogany wine rack near the bar and carefully he extracted a bottle.

At the bar, he uncorked the cool green bottle, filling two goblets. The ruby wine shown like blood through the crystal bowls as the firelight licked them. Then he moved to Keith with his new offering.

"Keith," Nicholas said softly, invitingly.

Lowering his eyes, Keith looked at the sparkling glass, the imprisoned liquid garnet, held in Nicholas's hand. "Thank you," Keith said graciously and almost as softly as Nicholas.

Neither of them moved.

They looked deeply then into each other's eyes, as though they were lovers, as if in that moment they had connected in a way where words and thoughts have no meaning, have no existence.

Nicholas's heart began to race, and although he was across the room, the fire seemed to consume him with unbearable heat.

It is the fire, Nicholas thought.

"Nicholas," Keith parted the silence, "were you the model for Zeus?"

"No," Nicholas responded.

Keith continued, "You look like him. I mean, in the painting," his eyes suddenly shy.

"It's coincidence. You look like Ganymede," Nicholas finished and handed Keith the goblet. Then Keith took the glass into his strong veiny hands and drank.

I'm too close to him. Nicholas thought suddenly. *I need to move.*

Nicholas looked at Keith's thick pink lips, wet with wine. The young man's face was like an exquisite Greek carving, cut like a stela in smoky marble.

Then Nicholas drank from his glass, the wine, a perfume of roses and burnt wood.

The two of them moved to the sofa which sat before the fireplace. A kaleidoscope of fiery color played along its length. Nicholas led, Keith followed, and they sat together, placing the goblets of wine on the glass table before them.

Into each other's arms they moved this time. Soft fire shadows brushed their skin which became naked as robes fell away.

Outside, the snow and wind began to die. Through narrow icy windows gentle moonlight trespassed discreetly into the room in long vapory rivers of silver.

Their lips touched and their tongues met. Their hands explored each other's bodies, as if it were the first time such an exploration had ever taken place between two people.

And Nicholas and Keith became submerged into each other's wantingness, longing only for the satisfaction to fulfill and to be fulfilled.

Deep in the center of heaven, beyond the reach of mere earthly thought, Zeus took the cup from Ganymede, and drank.

11

∞

I have said my goodbyes to Keith, and he to me, enough times to make a high school girl puke.

It was an evening I won't soon forget; just a bit though, I wish that he lived nearby.

I saw tears in his eyes as he kissed me, as he moved his face away from mine, turning to walk out the door.

We exchanged telephone numbers and addresses, but since it is true that absence makes the mind wander, not the heart fonder, I know they will not be used.

Keith was a very sexy, very beautiful boy: *Shalom, shana punim.*

Of course it is warming up outside. All the snow has melted into dirty shallow here-and-there puddles. The sky, again clear and blue, smacks of spring. I think of the trees. In my mind's eye I see dead buds. The bright paths of early April flowers that I saw yesterday, lining some sidewalks like evanescent rainbows, have vanished to be sure. Mother Nature, The Big Fucking Bitch, has done it again. How endearing she is.

Yet I think, without that storm, last night might never have happened. So: Up Yours Mother!

I notice again, as I had last night, that I have messages on my answering machine. I haven't been tempted in the least to find out to whom they belong. Unlike most queens, I do not have a lover relationship with La Telephone.

One friend of mine, his name was Kurt, actually had his telephone surgically attached to his head. No matter where Kurt was, there was his phone. It was his best friend you see. He had: call waiting, call forwarding, three way calling, four way calling, dial a prayer, dial a fuck, dial an orgy!

One fateful night while Kurt was asleep, the cord of his phone got wrapped around his neck like a boa constrictor, and he choked to death a la Isadora Duncan. And that, as they say, is that. Dial a joke.

I think that the phone answering machine has been *the* greatest invention since toilet paper. One needs a phone, it's true. Like taking a shit, the nasty necessity is obvious. But what one needs more than the phone is the answering machine. Like the Lamb of God who takes away the Sins of the World, the Telephone Answering Machine takes away the Calls: they are both ass wipes.

I decide that it is time for the message unveiling. Who knows, it could be business.

12

∞

A beautiful young man, sitting naked and cross-legged on the floor, was bathed by a pale early afternoon sunlight that liquidly drenched his skin gold.

Just having arisen from late sleep, Gabriel sat on the mattress in his room, regarding the piece of paper on which Nicholas had written his telephone number.

He held the note in his hand with the same care and appreciation that would a jeweler for a precious stone. In fact, to Gabriel, this small fragment of white paper was far more covetable, more alluring.

Gabriel studied each of the seven numbers. Committing each facet of this flawless jewel to memory, he let them become one unforgettable unit in his mind. These seven separate numbers, this one magic key, bespoke of something thrillingly unfathomable. For to Gabriel, Nicholas represented and therefore embodied the possibility of a resurrection of happiness and hope, which for so very long had been extinguished.

Since Sebastian's death, Gabriel watched the world go by with a desultory eye. Oona had saved his physical life, but his soul languished. Imperceptibly, day by day, Gabriel withered just a bit. Like phantom increments being cut away from a fading ghost, Gabriel's spirit was becoming perniciously hollow.

Now there was this Nicholas, this antidote to his desolation. Nicholas became Sebastian to Gabriel, yet Nicholas was Nicholas as well.

Why, thought Gabriel, did he leave his number at all?

Gabriel knew, even before he wrote his note to Nicholas, that Nicholas would not. But he was wrong. There it was, late last night, when he came in. The apartment empty, Oona at work, God sleeping in the kitchen, and the note was on his dresser, under a pen from a bar called Force Majeure, a place that he hated; now, quite suddenly, it was a place that he loved.

Yet, he dare not call Nicholas, not now, not just then. His idea, he felt, would be to appear calm about it, assured and unhurried. He imagined Nicholas to be the type who hated pursuers and clingers. Gabriel was right on target much more than he realized. So intuitively, he just knew that it would be in his best interest to wait. Wait, at least until the next day, Sunday, to give Nicholas a call.

But as Saturday night drew deeper into itself, making the silence of the apartment and the aloneness there cut closer to him, temptation rose gnawing in Gabriel's mind.

He thought about going out, about going to a bar where he could be with others, immersed in their distractedness, yet he would be alone, by himself, to be there only to drink and momentarily forget.

Changing what he would wear twice, and then for a third time, he stared at himself in the cracked mirror over his old dresser. He looked down, again at the note, that he had placed on the dresser's scratched and worn top.

The small square of white paper seemed to glow there star like. He could *not* go out, he thought then suddenly. To him, as foolish as he felt it really to be, to go out now seemed like an act of betrayal, one of indiscretion and infidelity against his hope of a possibility.

Stripping for a fourth and last time, Gabriel threw the unwanted clothes onto a small pile that had quickly grown near his tiny closet.

Lighting a joint that he had extracted from a small box in the top drawer of his dresser, Gabriel took a giant hit. He lit the candle on the dresser and moved to turn off the bedroom ceiling light.

He dragged on the joint for a second time then snuffed it out in an ashtray. The room turned as he fell back onto the mattress; his naked skin touching the cool cotton sheet, tingled.

Whispering candle-shadows glowing up from the dresser moved like butterflies across the ceiling of his bedroom.

"Flutterbys," Gabriel said out loud to the shadows.

He laughed, pointing up to the sky as he watched the wind sweep the little birds out through the window.

His eyes trailed slowly with the birds in their flight to the cold bluish square of glass in the wall of the bedroom. There, his eyes met a cloudless black silk sky that was dusted with a spray of tiny rhinestones shimmering in moonlight.

He thought again of Nicholas. His hand moved over his stomach to his cock. It grew hard with his hand's embrace and the touch of this thoughts. Closing his eyes,

Gabriel imagined himself having sex with Nicholas, the beautiful man that he desired. He came quickly.

Then Gabriel fell deeply asleep having no dreams at all that night.

14

∞

It's Bloody Mary time I think, as I listen to the finale on my answering machine. One, a business call, delights the fuck out of me; the rest are *dreck*, except of course the one from Anais.

Anais. My dear pretentious friend Anais, gets her name from-- well who else? Anais Nin. She's a writer. A damned good one too, I must admit. She calls her work erotica for women, but it's sheer pornography, with panache of course. She's also a fag hag and a nympho (and aren't they all!), which is why they *are* fag hags to begin with.

Fag hags, I have discovered throughout the years, always seem to suppress *It* you see. But, they always want *It* too. *It*, as D.H. Lawrence, so without knowledge of his being camp, put it, is the Love Connection. It's what they want more than anything else. They are obsessed with the Love Connection much more than with the fags that they are hags to.

Most of them (all of them, maybe) weigh a ton. They are Earth Mothers in moo moos. They are the beloved women beyond zaftig, pedestalized in every gay bar throughout the world by their fag fans.

Fag hags are a phenomenon in themselves I have always surmised. Perhaps they should enfranchise themselves in organizations-- unions that's it! They, as a group, would become a new thing-- a force to be reckoned with. Can you see it! Fag Hags For World Peace. Fag Hags Fight Hunger. Fag Hags For Abortion. Fag Hags Against Catholic Guilt. The list is infinite.

Anais is my fag hag, and I love her dearly. She'd like to suck my cock, I know this, but that is where my love ends.

She was one of David's closest friends, before she became mine, and she's lived in Chicago for all eternity. Those cool San Francisco summers, when David and I would come to Chicago to sweat, we'd stay with Anais at her all-the-rage house in the Gold Coast.

A regular Perle Mesta that Anais, throwing one fucking party after another. You wouldn't believe who would show up!

I met film stars, who, you'd never suspect were gay. One, in particular, I actually saw getting sucked off in her upstairs bathroom by this blond kid who couldn't have been more than sixteen. The star had a bushy black moustache and looked like the Marlboro Man, and when I told David that I couldn't believe what I saw, he said he couldn't believe that I didn't know already. Politicians, Catholic priests, restaurateurs, newspaper reporters, even a black militant lesbian nun I met at Anais's soirées. What a riot!

Those halcyon days are no more, cannot be really, or will ever be again; too bad.

Anais was also my life saver, no doubt about it.

When David died, Anais came to San Francisco and spooned me up off the floor. What little there was left of me she helped to put back together again. I owe that fag hag my life. Maybe I should let her suck my cock.

Anyway, fag hags *want* the Love Connection, they really do. So I think to myself, then why do they hang around with gay men, and almost all the time? They're certainly not going to get *It* from them, at least not from many. It must be an affliction, or perhaps an addiction, who can be sure? Are there books, I wonder, concerning the Fag Hag Phenomena? Perhaps a study should be made, some funded investigation by some not for profit group. This would be a gem for the University of Chicago, absolutely!

I wonder too, as I think this, as I prepare that Bloody Mary: are there heterosexual men who hang around with lesbians? Would dykes even want that anyway? And if they did what would these men be called? Diesel Weasels, that's it!

Enough of this crap I think. Soon, Anais will be here, and her Sunday afternoon Martini must be concocted *au grand serieux*.

15

∞

As Gabriel stood in the bathtub, as a hot needle-jet of water showered stinging down upon him, he contemplated the telephone call that he would make to Nicholas.

Already having had breakfast with Oona, confiding in her his fear and his desire about what he wished to do, Gabriel decided that since Nicholas had given his number it was there to be used.

But what would he say? Frightened that he would say, or not say, the correct thing, Gabriel continued to repeat variations of conversations over and over in his mind: Hello, Nicholas, this is Gabriel. How are you? Oh, I'm fine thanks. I hope that I'm not bothering you. Nicholas. I'm really glad that you gave me your phone number, I didn't think that you would.

No, absolutely not! Don't be such a wimp, Gabriel thought to himself as he rinsed the shampoo from his hair. A cloying wimp would be the last thing that Nicholas would want to hear from.

He thought again about how he might proceed, as he dried himself, as he stared at his steam-flushed face in the bathroom mirror over the sink: Nicholas, how are you? This is Gabriel. Fine, thanks. I thought that maybe we could get together, tonight perhaps, for dinner or a drink.

Oh, Christ no! How presumptuous that would be, Gabriel thought.

Gabriel reconsidered what Oona had suggested. She was appearing in a play with her boyfriend Speed. The play would open Friday night at the Theater Building. Invite Nicholas as your guest for opening night, Oona directed.

Perhaps, Gabriel thought as he emerged from the steamy bathroom, that is exactly what he would do.

⚜

Gabriel stood before his bedroom window dressed in faded blue Levis and a teal green Polo shirt. Staring longingly out into space, his thoughts adrift, he mindlessly regarded the city scene: the spring sun hung wanly in the sky, winter's ghost milky white, his only guests the fleeting gossamer clouds transparently greeting him as he gazed down upon the huddled rooftops of the city.

Gabriel was like that sun. A fragile whiteness bearing the potential radiance of platinum. His associations, all distant and ephemeral, he longed for the near, the concrete.

While Nicholas was with Gabriel that one night, for just a moment, Nicholas had been granted permission to see within Gabriel that essence which he himself desired in another human being.

To Nicholas, Gabriel was an angel indeed, though incognito, the Gods had yet to unveil.

16

∞

He wants to invite me to a play, the little angel does. And I find myself intrigued and turned off all at the same time.

Anais thinks the whole thing *smashing*, but I, on the other hand, am not so sure. Anais knows about this play too. She's met the playwright at a few soirées, says he's uncanny, a real genius.

"This one's his best," she offers reverentially and adds that she's been invited to opening night as well.

What a riot I think! We'll dd-oo-uu-bb-ll-ee date.

The name of the play is *The Glamour of Evil*, and I can't help but to try and find the irony buried here. There is an irony here I'm sure, but I'm not quite drunk enough yet to figure it out. I offer Anais another Martini, and I make myself another Bloody Mary.

Anais tells me in her languid, brooding way, as I mix at the bar, that the play is about this ravishing thirty-five year old nun who's got very hot pants. She's supposed to look like some kind of Isabella Rossellini. Anyway, Isabella's a career nun, you see, who is also a psychologist. She's counseling a confused, rakishly handsome young priest who is having trouble dealing with CHASTITY. Now ain't that a bitch!

Sister Isabella, as the story goes, starts to act a bit less professional with Father Divine. She gets to know him in the biblical sense and ends up in the confessional telling him that she's got a little consecrated bun in the oven.

"You're not on the pill?" his shocked voice quivers as he queries.

"No," says she with a mother's stern pronouncement: "I'm a nun."

He is not prepared in the least for *this* mess. It's much too much for our young Bishop To Be. So he ends it all. And he commits his harakiri at the very same moment Our Lady of the Flowers is having an abortion.

Is this too much or what!

I decide, just then, to go. Anais has convinced me. This cannot be missed I think.

Anais also tells me that the priest is being played by this beautiful up-and-coming young actor from Winnetka. Speed is his name she says, and his acting style is something else, *riveting*, is how she puts it.

I've met him, I tell her, with all the excitement of excrement in my voice. He's Gabriel's roommate's boyfriend, I let her know, and I can see that that thrills her. She's thinking, I can see, that maybe she'll get the chance to meet him, to eat him: there is always an orgasm happening in this one's eyes.

Anais sips her Martini. She then says to me with the hushed voice of a conspirator, as I light a cigarette, while I sit down next to her on the sofa, "We must find out, darling, if this boy is *really* straight."

What Anais means is: is he really gay? That is what she truly desires, his gayness you see, because then

96

in her mind there could never be a chance of getting *It* from him.

Anais, as all really good writers do, hates herself. She's fat, no doubt about that. She's an alcoholic (but then remember, Christ's first miracle was to turn water into wine because just how much fun is there without that divine grape juice?). She's much too sensitive to her environment, but that is why she is a writer. She can be wildly loud and obscenely clever, which is why she is Fun City. And she would, for her friends, those few that really are her friends, probably give her life.

Yet she can't get a fuck! And that is what she is desperate for. But because she hates herself wrongly, Anais is trapped in that pathetic web that so strongly paralyzes. She is, for all intents and purposes, a sexual paralytic. So I say, as another Great One has in the distant past: "*Talitha koum*, and get laid!"

I tell Anais what I know about Speed, which isn't much. But my suspicions are, that if you were to look into his wallet, you'd probably find the card to a lifetime membership in the Judy Garland Fan Club.

"Anais, my love," I say to her dryly, coyly, "she's far too pretty a thing to want to swim with fish." I wink at her, and she gives me an I'm-getting-fucked-up-on-this-booze-and-I-like-it smirk.

"Darling, what makes you so sure?" she drones quizzically. "You did say, did you not, that he sleeps with Gabriel's odd little Oona, the, oh how did you put it, *life saver*?"

Christ! Between this booze, of which I've swilled too much (they're probably triples because I AM the bartender), and this one's investigation into the Life and

Times of Speedohgodletmesuckyourcock, I'm *shvitzed*, which can only mean one thing: that it's time to play in the snow.

"A couple lines sweetheart?" I ask needlessly as I rise for the occasion to get the stash.

She grins a fat coprophagous grin and hisses, "I thought you'd never ask, you nasty little boy." She surprisingly looks very much like Divine in Pink Flamingos, and now I'm sure that they *were* triples.

Anais can be a greedy snow blower, and today, well, she seems especially in the mood. Not two, but four lines get sucked up that aquiline schnoz of hers. I, on the other hand, do two.

"Dar---ling," she breaths out after her last line, "this calls for another Martooni."

Handing me her empty glass with one hand, she rubs a bit of the old toot on her gums with a finger of the other. "Numb gums," she says, then says in a very fake German accent, "Now doktor. Now you can drill avay and I vont feel a thing." She laughs mirthlessly.

I can see numbing aloneness articulated in her eyes. And her eyes are shadowed by the grayness of despair. Anais is a deeply unhappy soul. I know this because I know that she is an empath. Her hell is forged from the hells of others, and that is the most inescapable hell of all. Vicariously Anais suffers, but she suffers for herself as well.

Leaning back she lights one of her every-now-and-then-long-thin-and-white-cigarettes which she keeps in a wafer thin mother of pearl case. The case is lined with gold. I catch its soft yellow glitter as she snaps it shut. Inside, there is an inscription from David. He gave it to her as a gift when she turned thirty. Shortly after that birthday, my dear Anais tried to kill herself. But she failed. Some things are just not meant to be.

I think sometimes about that, about how she almost died. And looking at her now, as I stand here at the bar preparing her drink, I am sure that one day somehow she will try it again. And I know, then, that she will not fail because she is a much stronger person than before.

It takes a great strength to commit suicide I think, a much greater strength than it takes to live. Yet, is it our own volition which gives effect to the cause, or is it something far more otherworldly that indulges our so called willed action?

Ah, who gives a shit? I think. Feeling good and drunk I walk back to the fag hag, sitting down next to her with her drink in hand. And as Holly Woodlawn once said to Geraldo Rivera, "What difference does it make anyway, as long as you look fabulous." I say this to Anais as she takes her cup of poison.

"And you look fabulous too, baby," she says as she sips and winks.

"Jesus."

Good and drunk, that's the thing. Who the fuck wants to feel bad and drunk? The coke just did the trick: the good and drunk trick.

"We must, darling," she is saying in a sotto voce slur, a slippery whisper steaming beside my available ear, "map our course, *capiche*?"

Her *capiche* is wrapped in a boozy breeze of breathless excitement.

"What the hell are you talking about, you old lush?"

"Old! Good Christ, Nicholas, such attempts at being loving."

She looks away from me with mock disgust. She speaks again, staring sharply into the Martini glass which she holds before her glazed eyes.

"We must figure these things out," she says cryptically, swirling the crystal glass. She is Madame Esmerelda magically gazing into her occult ball. What camp!

"We must unthread the mystery of your angel, and try to reveal the angle of my Speed."

She giggles like a lunatic at the end of this bizarre pronouncement. But that's only because she is one.

"Oh, God, this is too much! What the fuck have I done to deserve this?"

"Of course it is, you undeserving soul, much too much. You have met an angel, one that you have described quite clearly, and though you don't realize it, quite dearly. Me thinks, my boy, that you have indeed been bitten by the Smitten Bug. But you, Nicky Poo, are a selfish prig and can't see the forest fore the trees."

She eyes me with contempt; this time it's real.

"I think you mean prick, Esmerelda."

"Yes, that too."

An afternoon sun ray fell from a window gilting Anais's pewter hair. Her face mysteriously held lips attenuated, pensive. In thought the woman was beyond any I knew. In drunken drugged thought her mind was like the face of Medusa: deadly.

Anais's hair, like a tin nimbus, vibrated in the steamy sun-mist light. Her complexion, porcelain white, seemed translucent.

"Anguish is the result of a simple formula, Nicholas," she went on to say and stopped. Then went on to say to finish: "It is the byproduct of self-indulgent self-deceit. It is the rigor mortis of a once loving heart."

"My heart, sweetheart, the loving heart you so darken my door with, has long been on ice, shall we say. And because aloneness has been a perfect friend, I've had nothing but a real heart-on for quite some time." I say this with tongue in cheek and with the lack of drama that I suspect she so desires during this repartee.

"Your heart, Nicholas, is a lonely hunter, and when I look at you, when I really look at you, I see hunger and want in a face gaunt with the lack of love. I can smell that hunger in the air all around you."

I feel my hands tingle. Sweat is running from my armpits. She is opening up scarred over knife slashings. She is unearthing a sacred grave.

"Thank you, Dr. Brothers," I say and gulp down the rest of my drink.

"Nicholas, you need to get with it. You have to get over it! How long do you expect to play this depressing game of yours? Poor, slapped to the ground Nick."

She rises and moves to the window. Her back is toward me as I continue to sit. I close my eyes.

"Death *is* a part of life, you know," she informs me feelingly.

"Even you lack the elegance of sympathy, Dear One."

"If it's sympathy you're looking for, Camille, you can find it in the dictionary between shit and syphilis."

I open my eyes to fill them with the vision of the Wale Goddess who seems to know so much about death and life.

"Why don't you defenestrate, Miss Manners, and perhaps you'll accomplish what you once failingly attempted."

"I'll let that pass, Nicholas, because I know it's only the booze talking, but let me tell you this." She turns toward me and stops. "David is dead. No matter how much you drink, no matter how long you play this game of Mr. Freeze, of Mr. I Don't Give A Shit About Anything Anymore, you cannot bring him back. You have never forgiven yourself about being the survivor. I know that you can't understand why it was he and not you, but that's just the way things happen. Let him go Nicky and let yourself live. Would it be better if you both were dead?"

Shortly after David was diagnosed with AIDS, he developed PCP and almost died. That day David's doctor spoke softly to me. His voice, fatherly and urgent, undressed my illusions of this thing to its naked reality, while addressing the quickly approaching terms of finality. Why? I asked. We don't know, he answered. I asked this man of medicine miracles the whys and wherefores of my own health and physical integrity. You appear to be in excellent health, he said, and went on to say, your tests were negative, you have nothing to worry about. But this made me wince with worry. This made me feel worse. (Yet I had never felt physically better in my life.) I had been kissed by God, by God! So what demon, I thought, was kissing David? David was religious, a

Catholic, who as all good, I mean really good Catholics do, never missed Mass. But David was spiritual as well. His religion wasn't left behind on the altar when he walked out of that church. Christ no, he took it out with him into the streets! David helped the poor. On Thanksgiving day he would volunteer in some soup kitchen, while I would feign sickness or make up some excuse as to why I just couldn't go with him. He loved little children, especially the handicapped, and so he volunteered some time at the Children's Hospital. During the Christmas season he would visit this particular convalescent home for the senescent (the one where his grandfather had died) to spread the necessary Christmas cheer. David was joined at the hip with Jesus, unselfconsciously spreading the love of Christ to his fellow man. And I, selfish me, sat back in my comfortable chair, in my comfortable condo, comfortably reading my comfortable books or watching comfortable movies played on my expensive VCR. And where the fuck is David's God now? I thought, while my loving compassionate David was suffocating to death in some God forsaken hospital bed! Don't you see him God? I screamed inside: Don't you see your David, Jesus? The one who believed in you and spread your good word! *Why can't you help him now*? Yes, I thought, this is how I am to be punished. This is the answer to my sin of negligence. I am loosing my David, the only person I have ever truly loved like this. And I have been untouched by this leprosy. I have nothing to worry about. I am perfectly well.

Filled with tears, Anais's eyes touched by the sun, shimmered. I let my own tears escape. They ran down my face like drops of hot candle wax. She embraced me as she sat down next to me again, and like a little child who submits completely in the tenderness of his mother's arms, I cried with the unrestrained grief that I had never let surface.

17

∞

I have a very rich old friend named Matthew Landauer, who is also my business associate of a somewhat recent association, as is our friendship.

Matthew is a pornographer. But he prefers to be regarded as a maker of art films; a visionary, who lusts to visualize beautiful naked boys and men through a camera lens.

When in Chicago, Matthew stays at his swank two bedroom condo at 300 N. State Street, which is to say, Marina City. He has owned it for eons.

Matthew is also known by his intimates as Matinee. Having been summoned by Matinee, via the answering machine, to brunch with him, I prepare myself. I feel somehow that I must look my best. I always seem to get this feeling when Matthew calls.

This is of course a business meeting we shall be eating, and so to stimulate my non-existent appetite, I mix up a Bloody Mary.

My dinner with Anais, last night, did me in: Greek up the ass on South Halsted street. Like hot licorice steam, the bottle of Ouzo we split, is coming up on me. The tomato juice and Tabasco will kill that I think.

It is a sunny late morning. The irksome radio voice spewing forth bothersome babble has just informed me of the weather. Mid to upper sixties, possibly low seventies by afternoon, rain late in the day is probably a fact. She is also pandering some sentimental crap about the homeless. Something about the forty-sixth ward, a political activist named Helen Schiller, and *them* having nowhere to turn.

"Well hell," I say out loud as I carry my Bloody Mary to the entertainment center, "When you have nowhere to turn, turn on the gas." I say this as I turn Miss Rich Bitch D. J. off.

A CD is just the thing I think, as I slip the flat luminous bubble of classical gas into the slim black box.

Wagner!

I love the smell of vodka in the morning.

I sip my Molotov cocktail and head for la douche.

♟

I have arrived on the fifty-seventh floor, on time (which is expected), at Matt's circular abode. His pad, like a giant spying eye, floats high above the city. This eye, always open, stares down upon the shit-laden river of Chicago: the detritus of a city-gone-bad is pissed out to sea, forever moving past Matinee's unblinking heavenly eye.

The ivory door is opened by a smiling Johnny. This boy's dazzling white teeth would make even God jealous; they look like they're plugged into an electric outlet. Too perfect. Too much! My mouth begins to H20.

Johnny is Matt's Brazilian house-boy. But the Plain Truth I'm sure is, that this Ipanema Beauty is nothing more than a tight-assed fuck slave for Matinee's all too often primordial urges. It's a sad story, I think, as I move by Tall and Tan, sickeningly imagining Matt's pale little worm of a cock up Johnny's hot brown ass. *Tall and Tan.* If only he had a brain.

Mack The Knife, Matinee's mauve Manx cat, greets me at the door as well, sans tail.

"Pretty pussy," I say and pat the cat on its up-turned sniffing head.

"Nick-O-Lust," Matt breathes forth as he swirls around to greet me. He holds a pair of high-powered black binoculars in his long bony hands. His very tall slender form is aglow, backlit by the sun, as he stands before the almost invisible ceiling-to-floor windows of the living room.

"Matinee," I say, "voyeurism so early in the day? How are you, love?"

"Nicky, it is never too early to have a look see. Anyway, my dear, you know I am a camera. My eyes never close. I'm *wunderbar*! and you *Liebling*?"

"That's because you have no eyelids. You were born eyelidless in Gaza, a thousand years ago, beneath the Sphinx. I'm fine, just fine."

"Well, my dear, I may be of Egyptian ancestry, but I hardly think that I am that much of an antiquity."

"Don't be so modest, Matthew. Everyone knows that your birth certificate was painted on papyrus with dove's blood, not to mention the fact that it was you who authored that bestselling chapter of the New Testament-- in Cuneiform yet. Gin, Miss Landauer?"

"Lush. Johnny! What are you swilling down these days dearest?"

"J.B. and water. It's early, on the rocks please." I smile a vexatious little smile as I say this.

"Nick, dear boy, I must apologize, but the only scotch that I keep is Swing, Johnnie Walker's finest."

To the bar Johnny walks; smiling, he prepares the drink.

I sit down on a jet-black and gold velvet upholstered settee, immodest in length. How Cleopatra I think as I look around, again stupefied, by this all too soigné den of iniquity. So exotic is this strange pleasure palace that I feel my rectum twitch. It's absolute Cheops in a Kenneth Anger sort of way.

Johnny, moving toward the place where I have settled, swerves to avoid Mack The Knife, and serves me the Swing off a sparkling tray that goes with Matthew's silver service. His perpetual smile gives me reason to believe that the retarded truly can be happy. As he turns, this boy's tight little ass, wrapped in black denim, is proffered momentarily before my eyes. Then poof! like magic he and Ass A Go Go disappear, not to be seen again, until some other urgent avuncular plea shall arise out between Matinee's tense tonsils.

"Nice boy," I say to Matt as I sip my drink.

"How true, how very true!" he rejoins resoundingly.

"Yes," I say.

"And a marvelous cook."

"Cock?"

"No darling, you tease: *cook*!

"You'd never guess."

"Never! Ha, who could, not with those sweet little hot cakes dancing so gaily," Matt enthuses like a school girl with a hard-on. His watery blue bird eyes rise like helium balloons toward the ceiling as he continues, "Who would think such a beauty could be so down to earth domestic?"

Silently Matt slaps his thigh as he shakes his head, laughing lightly. Putting his giant black spy glasses in the top drawer of his desk for safe keeping, he sits down near to me, in a chair most unpleasantly overstuffed.

Lifting, off a decadent art deco side table, a skeleton's hand slowly brings to its mouth a tall champagne flute filled halfway with a colorless effervescent liquid. I can't help but think that the magician has performed the trick of levitation.

I can see the blushing imprints of Matt's thick lips near the rim of the glass. His lightly lipsticked lips (cherry pink on apple blossom white skin, powdered for sure) seem to be the only thick thing about his body. It's as if everything that is solid within him has come together in his lips, has congealed there contumaciously, spitefully recanting the exaggerated thinness of his overall self.

"How's your drink, old boy?" the old man questions paternally.

"Couldn't have made it better myself." I answer this truthfully. It's almost entirely scotch, the ice cubes swimming there simply to chill.

Akhenaton continues, "Saw a lovely site this morning through my dark looking glasses."

"Hmm. Mind if I smoke?"

"Oh, my dear, haven't you heard yet that that smoking business is so bad for you, not to mention so- *so* de´ classe."

"Matthew, spare me the homily on health and chic," I say, pulling a Salem out of its pack. I light it. "This is nothing compared with some things, dearest."

"If you must. Johnny! Ashtray please."

And just like that, that's it: over and done with.

"About your lovely sight?"

"Mmmm. Well, you see, I was standing out on the bedroom balcony early this morning. Mister Ra, the sun you know, had his sleepy eyes just slightly apart so everything was simply glowing a subfusc tangerine, the very color of sulfured pomegranates. It was very chilly. S-o-o-o refreshing when one has just been resurrected from his little death.

"Of course I just happened to have my binocs with me. I never leave the sarcophagus without them. (He laughs slyly.) Now you know, my dear, that the master bedroom here faces *that* other tower, over there (he refers to the west tower of Marina City as though it were a pariah). So I never feel intimidated in the least to see what troublesome things might be going on across the way. Really Nicky, it's very Sodom and Gomorrah, let me assure you. Well, let me tell you what these inquiring eyes beheld, dear Nick-O-Lust: A lad and his magic lamp!"

Suddenly I feel like I am in store for the one thousand and one mornings of one ancient Egyptian knight. But the Swing soothes me so.

"Yes, there he was, in all his steaming masculine glory! This tall nakedtanrippling young-- *young* Rajah, standing positively pompous before my high powered eyes, with his-- *his Dear God*, enormous cock fully erect, throbbing most indiscreetly in his giant hand!

110

"My dear! you can imagine my knees almost buckled right then and there, fifty-seven ups in the air. Oh, delicious vertigo!

"And this, Nicky old boy, is the kicker. This young lad saw me seeing him, and he liked it! Not ashamed in the least, this naughty boy was getting off on my, oh how shall I say, my observation, rubbing that pulsating pink piston, poker red, just for me. Can you imagine! I wanted to run for the video camera, but well, too late. The harder he rubbed, the hotter he got until, Allah be praised! out shot the genie all over the window! What a finale. Poor me, I was just drained."

"Oh, holy Moses, Matilda," dryly saith I. "If you can't take the sodom baby, you better get the hell out of Gomorrah." I let just a flicker of a smile burn momentarily at the corners of my mouth.

"Hmm." Sniffing with counterfeit agitation, Matt again takes a sip of his bubbling elixir. "I thought you'd enjoy my story, *Sahib*. I was certain that it would appeal wildly to your so well developed sense of salaciousness."

"*Sari, sarong* number *Sayyid*. And you did say that this was a business meeting?" I am not impressed with Matinee's story; they all sound alike.

"Ah, business. Yes, yes, but there is far too much business in this world, Nicholas. Alas, business always before pleasure; but then, our business *is* pleasure. It is our hap-*penis*." He smiles. It is the curled-lips-and-bared-teeth-smile of a dictator. The grimace of one who imagines himself imagining himself a legend. And what becomes a legend most? Black Humor.

"I have a vision, my dear boy. A dream," he continues dreamily.

I light another cigarette then take a swig of the Swing. Matthew's eyes are closed as he talks. I study the spider web of purple veins crisscrossing like the canals of Mars on his thin, almost transparent, brown eyelids.

"There is one thing that I wish to accomplish before I die, Nicholas. I am a filmmaker. Albeit, one of limited fame, yet one of unquestionable genius."

This cannot be denied I think. He is speaking about one hell of a gifted artist.

"We are living in a time of unspeakable misery--an age of abject sorrow. An era of great shining liberation suddenly and so unnecessarily has been reduced to a cinder pile of suffering and fear. Desire and Passion scream for their murdered sister, Fulfillment. What have we here but the matrix from which springs those same devils that arose out of the box of Pandora. A suffocating Chaos held secret within the bosom of Eros awaits darkly, seething to betray and make victim his Lover. Cupid is no longer that innocent babyfacedcherub shooting arrows with delicious sting. No, no alas he has become the Incubus, donning Satan's mask and seducing the world with a deadly pitchfork. His bailiwick is Darkness; his precinct Death. And it seems to me so much of the time these days, dearest Nicholas, it really does I am afraid, that Hope no longer springs eternal."

It is a lugubrious, overdone proclamation, though one with which I cannot disagree.

"What is it Matthew? What is it that you wish to do?" Truly mystified I ask this of him.

"I wish to make a great film. *The Film*. A motion picture overflowing with passion and light and the innocence of love *unlost*, as it was once so very long ago: *as I knew it*.

Matthew slowly opens his eyes. They are filled with tears, I see. He has moved himself to tears, dear old man, whose aging brain is filled with tears and with the flowers of the lost garden of LOVE which those tears have watered.

He wants to go back to that garden, that Garden of Eden he seems to know so well, so long ago. But, I think, what possible difference would it, or could it make now? No matter what, he'd still have to bite into The Big Apple, and I don't mean New York! We all would for that matter because you see: it's in the script, kids.

"Seriously Nicholas, this is my prayer," Matthew offers seriously. His hands tremble with a delicate palsy like rustling autumn leaves brushed by a breeze on a sleeping tree.

"Matthew, my dear," I say, "you do know, do you not, that more tears have been shed over answered prayers than unanswered ones?"

"Thank you *sweet* Saint Therese Capote!" he returns with geriatric verve. He's quite with-it I think.

"You know Nicky, the problem with all of you young boys today, is that you are all soveryjaded. But then, I suppose it comes with the age," he says breathing out a controlled sigh of ersatz melancholy. I know him too well; it's the same old shtick.

"Really, Matilda? You mean thirtysomething?"

"I mean the *age*. This ice age in which we are all prisoners. Like giant frostbitten Mammoths, who appear as nothing more than tiny hairy flies sealed in glacial ice cubes, we all have been befouled by it. It's no wonder you are the way you are. There is no blaming the victims of war, the living victims who are the true casualties. Only sympathy shall suffice, *ein bisschen verstandnis,* and yet this too is all but nothing."

"*Quos deus vult perdere prius dementat*," I slowly drone this campily monotone, as an incantation discharged from the mouth of a mad alcoholic, which I most probably am.

"How tragic is the truth in that. Yet, I do believe Nicholas, that there is more to all of this than meets our mere mortal eyes."

"Something, you might say, too *too* transcendental for our pathetic little brains to handle? Something like: Well, you see, we must have the bad so that we might know the good-- the dark to see the light-- hate to feel LUV. Is that it, sweetie? Could this be the marvelous mystical metaphysics given us by that sure thing called God. And if it is, oh, how thrillingly responsible of *Him*."

The scotch is hitting me just right, right between the eyes, and I'm beginning to feel pissed. This conversation is going nowhere fast, that's for sure, and so I think it's my duty, a sacred obligation in fact, to alter its meandering course.

"Time for another drink," I invite, holding up an empty glass. "About your film, Mr. DeMille?"

"I think that it is terribly sad, my dear, dear boy, that you have so blatantly said goodbye to God. I can't really imagine the depth of your grief in having lost your David, but it seems to me that this tragedy, overall, is not one of divine injustice, but rather, one of a much more human nature."

The pit of my stomach is a chamber churning with a voluptuous nausea. I feel a Kafkaesque metamorphosis coming on; my compound eyes diamond cut, faceted to Holy See in all directions the immense nothingness of Divine Non-injustice.

In other words, I am about to puke on the priceless Persian rug seemingly sweeping endlessly out before me.

"Matthew, when it comes to God the bottom line is that we do have our differences. You choose to believe. I choose not to."

"Yes this is true, sad but true. However, you may choose not to believe in God, that is your prerogative, but God still believes in you."

"Yes, of course *you would* know this. I keep forgetting that you are really Moses, hallelujah! Or is that Mohammed? I can never keep those two bastards straight."

"Shameful! I should have you thrown over the balcony posthaste, you defamer of Prophets."

"Matilda, the only profits that you truly care about, or require for that matter, are the ones from the distribution of your suck 'n fuck boy films. Those other Prophets could go straight to hell as far as this is concerned."

"Irreverent and shameful, that's what you are Nicholas!"

"So be it. Now, what about your *film*?"

"Johnny, La Lush needs watering," Matthew spits, then continues, his voice softening, "You are young, Nicholas. I know that you have beheld suffering, have quite clearly been a participant. Yet, the suffering held in the orb of your eye is a speck compared with the torture of others."

My mouth salivates vitriol.

"How *can* you measure suffering, Matthew? To what depth does one need plummet to be given the Truly Tortured Award? And what on earth dares *you* to believe

115

that you have this power to judge? I suggest, dear one, that you remove the plank from your own clouded eye first."

Hurt pours over Matthew's face, very suddenly, like a river of red wine spilling across a white marble floor. I am almost shocked by my own vituperative lashing, yet I do not feel guilty; the old man deserved it I concede.

Johnny has been standing silently next to me, and like a still life on canvas, he holds my new drink, motionless, offering. I really need this one bad I think. Taking the cold rock glass in hot hand, I look up smiling. For the first time, I see, that he is not.

"Well," I begin, breaking the icy and unacceptable gang silence. I look back to Matthew, into his stern cool cornflower blue eyes. "His master's voice. He hears it not," I finish. Smiling peevishly I sip my drink.

Johnny departs to parts unknown.

"Why must you be so hateful?" Matthew questions in a way that is almost in spite of why he interrogates. Without permitting my participation in this now reopened competition, he continues, "Hate and cruelty seem to be something very natural about you, something elemental, as dense as lead, imbed in your personality. Strangely enough, this is what partly draws me to you, magnetically. And it frightens me deeply, it always has, from the moment my eyes met yours. Because you see, in you Nicholas, I can regard the hell of my past."

"What is hell, Matthew?" I interrupt his Jungian spiel and light another Salem. I am amused, truly.

"Hell can be many things, my dear. For me, my hell is one of which I am barely able to speak," he renders, pausing. Genuinely transfigured by some terrible darkness that has seeped out of his past, his skin glows ashen.

"In my youth," he continues, "horror, like some incredibly expensive yet unimaginable distasteful liquor, intoxicated me. This horror, of which I tell you now, to which submission was the only possible means of escape, was a chilling madness into whose hands I fell prey through absolute willingness. It was the triumph of betrayal against myself. I sold my soul to the butcher to live among the butchered.

"Nicholas, this is something I rarely speak about, yet it never leaves my mind."

I nod my head. I can say nothing.

"My father was a German Jew married to an Arabian woman, who was my mother. This man, my father, was an intellectual, a business man who, with my mother, a music teacher, lived in Germany. It was during the rise to power of Adolph Hitler that that madness, of which I tell you about now, opened its ugly, ugly eyes.

"Like two giant spotlights sending forth beams of black ray, these hideous eyes stared at the world with a dreadful, devouring, and ugly self-confidence. This ugliness, perverted by a villainous glamour, became somehow alluring and beautiful. And this madness looked upon *me*, Nicholas, my father's and my mother's pretty young son. It looked upon me with a dazzling gaze so calculated and absolutely cold. With complicity I responded to this dazing flirtation, and into its eyes I stared back: because you must understand, there was nowhere else to look. What did I see when I gazed into those hypnotic eyes of captivation, my love? A chance not to die! I saw the chance of a possibility in the eyes of the murderer, who courted me. And His eyes were sincerely Blue, like the Heavens of Germany; His hair was Golden Blond like its Son. His face, not unlike your own, gave me a strange reason to believe, while His blushing lips secretly whispered: '*Ich liebe dich.*'"

"I love you," I say.

"Yes. That is exactly what He said: I love you, '*Ich liebe dich.*' He said this as He eviscerated my father, who was an intellectual and a business man, and above all, a German.

"He said, I love you, as He dismembered my mother: the musician, the artist, the Arab. He did these things before my eyes, and around me I saw all of them, all my fathers and mothers succumb to His love. I love you, He said to me, '*mien Liebling,*' again and again, while I, genuflecting willingly before Him, sucked His cock, or gave Him my ass to fuck, or my beautiful young face to slap and be spat upon at His whim. Whatever He demanded, this Aryan god, I gave to Him thankfully. And all the while He never stopped saying: '*Ich liebe dich.*'"

I am shaking, yet desperately I try to conceal my shock at the implacable gravity of Matthew's terrifying revelation.

"Look," the old man offers, his voice a tender whisper. Slowly, his hand as stilled as a surgeon's, Matthew pulls up the long silk sleeve of his blouse. At first I see a tattoo, but then, I see a line of black numbers indelibly etched in the pale flesh of his thin hairless arm.

Horror falls upon me, now most audaciously pronounced.

I pull my eyes up to meet his, yet not wanting to.

"Look," he repeats through a smile, "this is the number of my life. It is the address of the whorehouse that was once my home. And we all know, Nicholas, do we not, that home is where the heart is." He finishes this with a cynical twist to his voice. It is a strange and frightening non sequitur I think.

My mouth is dry and a queer arrhythmia has seized my heart. All feelings, bad and good, have fallen away from me, out of me, leaving me emptied with only the cold prodromal touch of possible impending unconsciousness.

"I am so very sorry," I say to Matthew. I finish my drink in a swallow. It keeps me from choking on the tears in my throat.

"I don't know what to say," I say softly.

"Say nothing, because that is all you can do."

Deeply touched with anguish and humility, I do as I am told.

Accompanying my host in silence, we move to the dining area, and seat ourselves for lunch.

18

∞

"In the concentration camp," Matthew promises through a mouthful of blackened amberjack, "you try not to remember life. You *do* remember life, do you not, Nicholas?"

"Yes," I say, putting fork to fish, "I do."

Johnny sits across from me at the long glass top table; Matthew reigns at its head. So attentive to Matthew's every need, is Johnny, that I think at any minute he'll start feeding the old man.

"*Liebling,*" Matthew turns an admiring face toward his love, "most delicious, as always."

He lets his smile linger for just a moment longer than his compliment. His eyes reminisce with Johnny's in some secret understanding.

"*Danke, mein liebe Herr,*" Johnny responds, in perfect German, which is said in a way that sounds perfectly rehearsed. The eerie rendezvous over, old eyes roll back to mine coolly demanding my attention. I sip my wine.

"This world is not this world, my dear Nicholas. It is an optical illusion of unthinkable proportion, which only through the lens of madness can its true shape and size be surmised. And then, yet, in just a very limited way."

"It is a riddle, wrapped in a mystery, inside an enigma, thus spake Zarathustra," I say as I bite into a firm stalk of very fresh, very green, sweet asparagus.

"That was Churchill, dear boy, not methinks Zarathustra."

We both smile. The chill in the air lifts.

"Madness, you say?"

"Yes, of course, madness. Everything revolves around it. Is firmly rooted in it. It is the gravity of life itself, its mystery if you will, and as you shall recall, you *do* remember life."

Matthew at once regards my quizzical expression in response to all of his rambling. I'm sure he can see in my face, that I know, that he knows his elevator doesn't go all the way to the top. Nuts always know this.

"Take for example: *God*," the old man offers evocatively.

"I'm all ears," I say as I stick another stalk of asparagus into my mouth.

"For God so loved the world," Padre Landauer's eyes close as he breathes forth this incantation, "that He gave His only begotten Son." He, His, and Son all come out a bit louder.

"Johnny three sixteen," I say.

"Pardon?" says Johnny.

"Quiet," Matthew intones, then continues. "That God should offer Himself for destruction at the hands of His own creation, is this not madness? Divine Madness! And that through this act alone, through this glass darkly, has God and Man become one: perfectly reconciled. The very scary truth of the matter, Nicholas, is that God made Himself man so that man might make himself God."

"Force majeure personified!" I tap the crystal water goblet with my knife. "What a challenging idea," I enthuse with mock adulation.

"I couldn't have said it better, dear boy."

"But Matthew, I thought you were a Muslim. What's with all this Thomas Aquinas crap?"

"Yes-- yes I am. A Muslim, a Jew, Christian. It makes no difference. God, dear Nicky, has revealed himself to many people in many ways. Because you see, that *is* the way of God: madness. Madness is God's way."

"Matinee, my love, I do have a strong feeling, really I do, that La Popessa there yonder in Vatican Land, would take you to task over this new age catechism of yours."

"Nicholas, you do not have to believe in the Pope simply because he pretends to be holy. Nor do you have to believe in an ayatollah, Khomeini or otherwise. They are, in the end, just people like ourselves, sometimes better, sometimes much worse."

"And so Matthew, with all due respect, where was your God when all of your mothers and fathers came to their mutually untimely end on Earth, under the god-like hand of Mr. Hitler?"

"In my heart, Nicholas. Always in my heart. You see, God is where the heart is."

"I thought home is where the heart is?"

"God *is* home."

"And there's no place like home," I say smiling and finish the wine in my fingerprint stained glass. Lovely Johnny does the refill trick.

"Thank ya homie," I offer.

"Pardon?" Questions a wide-eyed Johnny.

122

"Thank God. For the refill, dear Johnny."

"You are very rude, young man." Matthew holds back the beginnings of a smile.

"That I am." I sip my wine. "That I am."

Johnny plays maid. Very tactfully he orchestrates the clean up routine. I can tell, just then, that coffee is on the way.

"Johnny," says Matthew to Johnny, "If it has warmed up outside, we'd like to have coffee on the terrace, *bitte*."

"Of course, *mein Herr*," Johnny respectfully responds, vanishing into the kitchen.

"Well trained." Pleasantly, I give voice to my observation.

"He is not a dog, Nicholas."

"No-- oh, Matthew no. Surly you misunderstood my remark."

"Miss Shirley Understood," Matthew says as he stands, "once a devoted secretary of mine and Mr. Herr, remarked how remarkable it was in the way that he and I resembled the other. Surly, Miss Understood I said, you can see that there is nothing remarkable here at all. Nothing at all, except perhaps what a *well trained* eye might observe. But, *mein Herr* she said to me and Mr. Herr: you cannot teach an old dog new tricks. What remained to be seen is that Miss Shirley Understood misunderstood that blood does indeed look much thicker than *Wasser*."

Matthew smiles a queer crooked smile. His eyes remind me of those of a brightly lit jack-o-lantern. I suddenly feel oddly disturbed, as though his telling smile and weirdly pronounced tale of word play mean a lot more than I can, or desire, to deduce.

"Excuse me, Nicholas, while I visit the you-know-what. And do make yourself comfortable outside, if that is in fact where we shall be."

I also need the you-know-what I think, but I can wait.

Through the living room windows I see that Johnny is preparing the green astro-turffed balcony. His short black hair, streaked with bright sunlight, has a glassy radiance that catches my eye. Under the thin white cotton shirt that he wears, I watch the muscles of his back and shoulders move as he works. This shirt fits him tightly, and the dance these muscles do cannot be missed. His skin is brown, but not from the sun. His skin is smooth and hairless; there is not even a small wrinkle on his Semitic looking face. He is very beautiful, I think, as my cock grows hard, painfully trapped by my underwear. I stand and adjust things.

"Got warmer," I say to Johnny as I walk out onto the large semicircular terrace.

"Yes. A beautiful afternoon, after all." He smiles looking up at me as he arranges fresh flowers in a glass vase on the table.

I study the blue veins running the length of his nicely defined arms.

"You work out I see," I compliment.

"Oh, yes," Johnny says with a hint of a modest laugh.

"I used to too. When I lived in California."

"You gave it up?"

"Yes."

"Looks like you still do," he says sincerely and moves to pour coffee into two cups.

I sit down in one of the chairs that sits beside the round wrought iron table.

"Beautiful china," I say observing the black coffee cups.

"Mikasa," Johnny offers informatively.

"The coffee smells exquisite," I say.

"Blue Jamaican," Johnny rejoins.

"We are," comes the voice of the old turtle, "drinking Blue Jamaican coffee from black Mikasa china cups," Matthew's voice from behind explains.

"*Tres chic!*" I ejaculate, then rise to take a piss.

"It's off to the old johnny for me, old boy," I say to Matthew as he sits.

"Oh, *scusi, bella donna,* didn't mean ya no harm," I say to Johnny and wink as I dash to the can.

⇧

"One cannot truly cogitate the overwhelming reality of the holocaust, unless one has been a participant." Matthew says this to me reflectively as he refills his coffee cup with the steaming black brew.

Johnny having done his disappearing trick again, leaves us to fend for ourselves. A bottle of vintage Armagnac has been placed on the table, I see, along with two crystal snifters. I can't wait for the invite to pour. Really, I can't, so I say to Matthew, "Shall I?" as I wave my hand gesturingly toward the toffee colored bottle.

"Of course, dear boy, please do, we both could use it," Matinee says cheerfully.

"Matthew, you are indeed the arbiter elegantiarum," I say as I uncork the bottle and dispense the booze. And what booze it is!

"This is absolutely wonderful, who could have guessed!" I gush.

"Oh, thank you dear boy, it is dreadfully expensive. I rarely do drink it, and of course, never alone."

Too bad for him I think. If I had this cat's money, I'd drink it every chance I could, and always alone.

"Really, Matthew, such restraint. I admire that."

"Restraint is the first step toward extinguishing desire."

"Your new philosophy, my seeker of wisdom and truth?"

"Oh no Nicholas, a very old one. In fact it was Shakyamuni the Buddha who made it clear that desire is the source of all suffering."

"Hmm, gee I thought that suffering was the *cause* of desire. I mean, if you're living in some stinking rat infested hell hole, and ain't that sufferin' man, you just might be motivated to get your ass someplace better. Like right here," I say grinning.

"Quite true, quite true. We have just created the notorious vicious circle, now haven't we?" Matthew announces somewhat apologetically.

"You were saying something about the holocaust."

Pleased to see that an ashtray has been placed upon the table, I light a cigarette.

"I said, that one cannot understand such things, ultimately, unless one has been there. One also cannot

126

know the unspeakable peace of salvation, unless one has been saved."

"I see," I say.

"And I have been saved," says Matthew. "In more than one way."

"That sounds cryptic." Smoke comes out of my mouth with the words.

"It is more than that," Matthew's voice grows tight with seriousness as he raises one white lattice of an eyebrow.

"In the concentration camp, I was a very young boy. Very beautiful was I, my beauty not unlike that of a girl's. A great deal of homosexuality existed in the camp, especially between the captives and captors. One high ranking Nazi camp administrator took an instant liking to me. He brought me to live with him, as his servant so to speak. This Nazi god loved young boys, you see, and I became his little *pipel*—his angel. He had others, of course, but I was always his favorite. And I was the only one permitted to live with him."

"This was your salvation?" I query.

"Yes and no. This man's name was Ernst. He was, in fact, a very good, kind man. He too, was very beautiful, physically that is. The perfect Aryan god. Ernst was an occultist, a mystic. Quite a bit of that went on then, in Germany. Hitler himself was deeply involved in the occult, you know. Once Ernst spoke to me of Hitler's obsession to possess a talisman called the Spear of Destiny. This, Ernst had told me, was the spear that the Romans employed to pierce Christ's chest as he died on the cross. Ernst said that whomever possessed this spear could control the destiny of the world."

"He did, did he?"

"Yes, he did indeed."

"Well, Matthew, if Hitler hated the Jews so much, why on earth would he believe that a stick, stuck into one, would do anything at all. Unless, of course, he really did believe that the Jews were in control of the world. You know what I mean, all of that business about a well organized conspiracy of Jewish bankers and communists out to control it all."

"Nicholas, dear one, Hitler did not believe that Christ was a Jew at all. He believed he was a Catholic."

"I thought he was a Protestant."

"Hitler?"

"No, darling, Christ."

"Very amusing, Nicholas. *Hitler* was a Catholic. He had strange and twisted ideas about religion. Ernst had told me that before Hitler became the Fuhrer, he was a member of a dissident occult organization called the Thule Society, which was a prefigurment of his Third Reich."

Matthew stops and sips the sun-brushed caramel colored liquid in his crystal glass. Something about his story sounds strangely familiar. Very 20/20 I think.

Meister Landauer continues, "The Thule legend, Nicholas, is as old as the German race, older perhaps. Thule, you see, was a lost island that supposedly existed somewhere near Labrador. The legend has it that Thule was the sacred magic capital of a vanished civilization."

"Yes, Virginia, there was an Atlantis!" I interrupt enthusiastically.

"Impertinent little swine," Matthew smiles. "Hitler and his cronies in the society believed that they were in possession of Thule's secrets. These people, Hitler and so on, had been influenced by the thinking of a strange and physically ill writer named Dietrich Eckardt. Evidently, it was Eckardt who had been instrumental in orchestrating the machinations of this small but powerful clique, capturing Hitler's ripe attention, and making him a member.

"Adolf Hitler became Dietrich Eckardt's protégé. It was he who helped to shape Hitler's Aryan doctrine concerning a master race of German super beings that would enable Germany to dominate the earth. Hitler became a dying Eckardt's instrument-- Eckardt saying before his death, to the few first members of the embryonic Nazi party: 'Follow this man for it will be through him that I shall lead.' Eckardt died not too long after the National Socialist Party had been formed in nineteen twenty-three."

"*Heil Hitler*! Very spooky, Matthew." I sip from my snifter. "Isn't it true that the swastika was some sort of occult symbol?"

"Yes, yes indeed it was. An ancient Indian cross."

"Sheets or feathers?"

"What on earth?"

"The Indians. Sheets or feathers?"

"From India. Nicholas you are incorrigible. Hitler was also a strict vegetarian."

"And I thought he was a cannibal."

"That he was, dear boy." Matthew slowly shakes his head sadly. "That he was." He sips his cognac.

"Ernst. What else?"

"Yes, Ernst. Ernst told me that he had seen the face of God-- that he had spoken with Him."

129

Matthew captures my eyes with his. His pupils are pin points, and the cold blue irises are drizzled with a thousand tiny storms of suffering.

"What did Ernst say that God had said?"

"He said that God told him: 'Joy is a river ceaselessly flowing.'"

"Hmm. Yep, that sounds exactly like something God would say," I say, and finishing my elixir, I pour another.

"You don't understand, do you Nicholas?" Matthew lowers his voice.

"What, Matthew, is there to understand? Hey, if God says that joy is a river ceaselessly flowing then by God I'll drink to that." And I do.

"You couldn't possibly understand. How could you?"

Matthew turns his face away from me and gazes through the black wrought iron balcony railing. A train of low floating clouds cuts across the Sears Tower's antenna with slow locomotion.

Not at all eager to pursue Ernst's God's mystical announcement I change the subject a bit, "Your salvation. You must tell me Matthew."

"No, I don't think I shall," he says looking back at me. Immediately he continues, "It was in the concentration camp that I came to understand Adolf Hitler. His struggle became *mein kampf*, my struggle, that is, to live. And it was there that I learned of another of God's promises: Work shall make you free.

"I was young, true, but I could work, and so, narrowly did I escape death. My parents--" Matthew's eyes swell with tears, "were not so fortunate, Nicholas. I saw

130

them, my mother and father, their naked bodies standing before faceless monsters who brandished machine guns. Along with countless others, I watched them jump into deep trenches of raging fire. This is Hell, I whispered numbly, losing sight of my mother and father as all of them, slowly consumed by the inferno, met their hideous premature death.

"Right after that I became a tortured slave. And my eyes have seen things that my lips cannot utter." Matthew finishes his dreadful account, and looking down he lovingly lifts Mack the cat, who has come to visit, to his lap.

"Your life," I say to Matthew, "even though you survived, I can't imagine it not being destroyed."

"But you forget that I was saved," he says this to me almost blissfully as he strokes the sleepy faced cat that has curled into a ball on his lap. Suddenly I think that he looks very much like that cat. Twin sets of eyes that have been narrowed through a mutually induced hypnosis of hand on fur.

"You were saved by Ernst," my question a statement.

"Ernst rescued me from the slavery of the labor camp. And he spared me from the finality of the gas chamber. Because of Ernst, all I knew then was the smell of the ovens.

"But Ernst too, did not come without the pain, without that carefully metered measure of abuse and degradation so easily laid upon the victim.

"I became for Ernst his chosen, and yes, his willing *nafka*. Do you know what this means, Nicholas?"

I say nothing; yes, I know what this means.

"It is Yiddish for whore. I was his little ten year old whore who willingly gave himself, no matter how much pain or shame, in exchange for my life. And yet, how unsure I was, of that.

"Ernst was a young man compelled by strange pleasures. He liked to sodomize little boys, and he also liked to be fisted by them, but these things were hardly the most exotic of Ernst's repertoire. It was I who was picked for that."

Matthew eyes me in a curious way, as if he thinks his story too provocative to continue.

"Shall I continue?" he asks.

"I don't see why not, the truth is best," I say.

"So true. Ernst," Matthew goes on, "had a fetish, you see. *Very dark*. He was a shit eater, Nicholas."

Nervously, I almost laugh out loud, but I suppress it. I wonder if the old man really knows what he has just said?

"I cannot continue, my dear, for it is just too upsetting," Matthew says, his voice slippery with the pitiful melancholy of an old lady's.

Mack The Knife, rising, performs his demonstrative feline stretch, and jumping off Matthew comes to rest silently on the balcony.

"Oh, my dearest Nicholas," Matthew sighs heavily, "it takes music to make the devil humble."

"Pardon?" I say, as I touch Matthew's glass with more cognac.

"Ernst always said that it took music to make the devil humble. Ernst played the violin. He could have been a master, my *beautiful* Ernst."

Matthew, very briefly, catches my eyes with his. His eyes, sudden with concern, look as if a great secret has slipped, which, undoubtedly, I think, has.

"Matthew, really, if you don't--"

"No, I-- I *have* to speak of these things; to you, my dear one, I must give my heart."

"Why to me, Matthew?"

"Because, you so remind me of Ernst. You are most probably his reincarnation. I know, Nicholas, that you must think me quite mad and all, but Ernst-- he brought me to God."

All the color drains from Matthew's face and he becomes, for the moment, a ghost.

"To God?" I ask.

"Yes, dear boy: *to God.*"

Matthew and I do a duet in sipping our liquor. *How does a Frenchman hold his licker?* (The old joke slips through my brain just then.) *By the ears,* of course.

"Tell me then," I say and light a Salem.

"Ernst," Matthew begins, and standing he walks to the balcony rail, "had the power, if you will, of ambulation outside of his body."

He turns and stares at me. Slowly, Matthew moves in a circle around the balcony as he speaks. He reminds me of a drugged moon in a Valium orbit. Soon, the waning moon, is behind me.

"Astral projection? That's what you're talking about isn't it?"

"Yes, I suppose that is what some have named it. Ernst could do this at will, whenever he desired you understand.

"Many times, and there were many times, I would find Ernst in deep sleep upon his bed, yet only to receive reports of him moving about, somewhere else, in the camp. These reports too came not just from within the camp, Nicholas, but from places far away."

"Sounds to me like Ernst had a bad case of bi-location."

"What I tell you is the truth, Nicholas. Every word of it," Matthew decrees as he waxes yet once again before my eyes.

"You really should sit down, Matinee, or soon you'll need a Dramamine."

"Yes, dear boy, a good idea. A good idea indeed," Matthew says folding himself into his vacant chair. "Ernst, though truly a tortured man," continues Matthew, "was absolutely unrestrained by the fetters of this world."

"Prometheus unbound!" I declare.

"*Ein bisschen von verstandigung, bitte,*" der Alter Mann exhales limply.

"Sorry, *mein Herr,*" I say while extinguishing my cigarette.

"As I said before, Nicholas, Ernst was a mystic, one of the cognoscenti of forgotten, and to most, forbidden secrets. He had, and I know this for a fact, entree into The Other World." The Other World rolls around in Matthew's mouth with distinct initial caps.

"Sounds like a soap opera," I say.

Matthew leans stiffly forward as though he's about to reveal something very hush hush. "Ernst held the keys, you see. Not only could he unlock the door for himself, dear boy, he could unlock it for others as well." Relaxing again in his chair, Matthew displays a lean smile economic in emotion.

"Are you," I ask, "referring to the door to The Other World?" My question suggests the possibility of something else, which I know there is not.

"Yes, yes, yes," Matthew's affirmative trilogy a perturbed staccato.

"He opened it for you, then," I quickly offer.

"Most definitely. He opened the door for me, and I entered," he states, conspicuously moved by the memory.

Closing his fluttering eyelids, the eye whites just momentarily visible as if his eyes have rolled back into their sockets, the Sorcerer's Apprentice tells the tale.

"It was as if I were to be initiated. Older, was I, then, thirteen, and this was the magic age, Ernst said. 'You, Matthew, are no longer a child, you are a man.' Ernst, you see, had already made the promise of opening the door for me. Friday evening, that night of my thirteenth birthday, I entered Ernst's strange twilight world, and I beheld God."

I grow cold and a chilling tingle spreads down my back as I listen to Matthew. Not because of the content of his story (his story, weirdly like Gabriel's, however outré, strikes me as being fairytale naïve), but because of Friday and thirteen, the day, pathetically enough, on which David had died. I have, since then, avoided the number thirteen like the plague.

"That night, in Ernst's bedroom, a secret place at best thought of as a most private sanctum, the ritual began.

"I reclined naked upon the giant canopied bed. A fire in the small fireplace of the room defended me against the cold. It was a night pregnant with snow; my birthday being in February, wolf-voice wind sang without harmony outside the house. And on the window of that room I saw white crystal ice webs copiously spun by some invisible hand.

"Ernst instructed me to regard the great gold monstrance that stood majestically atop his armoire. He said that the golden vessel contained the consecrated host: the Body of Christ. I, being not of the Christian faith, was once unfamiliar with things such as this, but Ernst had been a good teacher, instilling in my young mind his philosophy, which was one abundant distillation of other brilliant thinkers as Rudolf Steiner, Madame Blavatsky, Aleister Crowley among many others and in all probability, Hitler himself, I am sorry to say.

"Ernst sat next to me as I lie on his bed, one so big that to my then small way of thinking, I felt as if I were floating upon an enormous cloud-filled barge. He touched my forehead, a delicate warm fingertip placed lovingly on a spot between my eyebrows. Quite suddenly, Ernst's finger, that just moments before was simply comfortably warm, grew hot with such intensity that I was transmogrified with an unexpected uncontrollable oscillation of humor and fear.

"Then this great heat transformed. No longer was it a blazing fingertip that I felt, but a current of pulsating electricity, a wave of cool liquid energy which, being directed into a carefully sought and found acupuncture point leading directly into my brain, numbed me into blissful paralysis.

"Before came the dream that was not a dream, Ernst dreamily whispered into my ear, *'Elagabalus, finis coronat opus.'* My eyes then closed, and I fell down through his bed and flew fluidly up into the blue-black night.

"Suddenly, I stood naked before a huge gray stone building. Eight enormous granite columns, their shape severely phallic, rose indecently upward where they supported its overhanging roof. The front of this edifice was approachable from a marble stairway which delivered one to its landing.

"I slowly ascended the white, hot steps. Above my head a blazing sun hung low in an ice-blue sky. As I approached the landing I became surrounded by a growing wave-like shadow spilling down over the steps. Looking up to the sky I saw a glacier-white full moon rising from behind the building; blood oozed from a vagina in its center. As the cold moon eclipsed the burning sun I felt a bloody mist sweep over my naked flesh.

"Upon reaching the landing I saw that my feet and hands had been pierced with vagina-slits; the wounds painlessly bleeding, imitated the bloody moon.

"Starting lightly-- angelically, I heard a symphony of voices sing a strange but delicate hymn. The two great wooden doors of the building, its mouth beyond the landing, opened. Entering, the voices of the chorus elevated in pitch as the giant doors slowly closed behind me.

"I stood in darkness. Oppressive emptiness confined me to that spot. Unbearable, the castrati voices soared into a cacophonous crescendo; just as unexpectedly, they withdrew, absolutely silent.

"I am lost, I said out loud. Lachrymosely, my voice echoed into the visible nothingness that surrounded me.

"Deep, so deep in the heart of the building, I heard the swell of pounding timpani. My heart, beating woefully, imitated the distant rhythm.

"Forced from the place where I stood, as if pushed forward by some violating power, I proceeded to move through the gauntlet of black emptiness.

"Hail Mary Full Of Grace, I murmured, Pray For Us Sinners Now And At The Hour Of Our Death.

"Distantly, the drums' reverberation seemed to grow heavier in my ears, and as I moved, summoned by the cadence of the drums, the sorcerous castrati chorus again began to sing: *Freude ist ein ewig fließender Fluss . . Freude ist ein ewig fließender Fluss.... Freude ist ein ewig fließender Fluss* .... JOY IS A RIVER CEASELESSLY FLOWING, until drum and song merged in a frenzied sonic embrace!

"Silence! Sudden overpowering silence. A presence, hidden from my eyes by the darkness, stood before me commanding the silence, yet, not a word had been uttered.

"Who are you? I asked, my voice that of a frightened mistrusting child, which I was.

"Almost undetectable at first, I smelled combustion. Something like the sweet resinous odor of church incense touched my nose.

"Fear in its full velocity roared through me then. And my eyes opened.

"Like a somnambulist, she moved toward me over the steaming ground.

"Her eyes were large oval glass orbs veiled by curtains of dark mist.

"Ensanguine lips.

"Her movement was as if she were on wheels-- very slow, vibrating now and then with delicate convulsions.

"Oh, she was so tall and sleek; her naked breasts, ruby nipples, dripped Holy Ghost Milk.

"The skin she wore seemed gleaming wet, serpentine, black patent leather infused with a cloisonné-crackling of gold.

"Her hair was golden honey and red poured through it, burning lava, its incandescence surrounded her face.

"Her vagina was hidden by honey and lava set deep within thighs of strength and beauty.

"She was before me.

"I moved to her, afraid to touch, as if she were heaven born. 'Suck from the breasts of The Virgin Mother,' she whispered as she took my head between her rose scented hands. Willingly, I placed my lips upon her breasts, to her nipples one by one, and did as she commanded.

"She moved my head away from her, and I saw as I gazed upon her face that her eyes were unveiled, each a glowing monstrance containing the Blessed Host, bearing the bleeding face of Christ.

"'I Am Saha The World Is Suffering,' stentorianly she intoned. And she took my right hand placing it against her left breast. With one clean swift movement of her other arm, her hand holding a silver scimitar, she sliced my hand off at the wrist. The hand furiously gripped her breast.

"I fell to the steaming earth, onto my knees, worshipfully looking up at her face, into her eyes.

"There was no pain.

"She removed the hand from her breast. The fingers of the hand extended themselves in an obscene stretch, and she set each fingertip on fire with her tongue.

"Holding the macabre candleabrum high above her head she proclaimed in a voice wrapped in thunder: 'This is the Hand of Glory pierced by the nipple of The Virgin Mother. It shall unlock The Door.'

"Clouds of white incense, heavy with myrrh, billowed upward into the vaulted ceiling as the hand burned.

"Genuflecting before her, my skin I saw gleamed as polished glass, shot bright by the powerful light.

"I looked down upon her feet, unshod. But, they were not her feet!

"The hem of the white robe, touching His ankles, wafted breezily. The sound of silence my ears detected, as I watched the fluttering cloth, was laced with hissing from the burning hand.

"I saw a rosebud resting tenderly upon each of His pale feet, the white robe never touching. How lovely, I whispered. Tears swelled in my hope-filled eyes as I bent lower. Moving my face near to each flower, I inhaled the perfumed blossoms. I kissed each rosy wound which opened, each crimson wound that bled upon His feet. The blood covering my lips tasted like sweet wine. And then I brought my eyes up to meet His face.

"Jesus Christ lowered His hand, helping me to stand. An amethyst nimbus of ethereal light glowed gently about His head. We gazed into each others eyes. My fear subsided.

"Permitting me to take the Hand of Glory into my hand that had been restored, Jesus said: 'This Is The Light Of My Heart That Burns For All Time,' His voice so righteous and irenic.

"I thought you had died, I said to Christ. I said, I thought all the Jews were dead.

"His face, suddenly sad, appeared so careworn and tired. 'No, my love.' He shook his head slowly from side to side, 'There is no death. This is what I came to tell you.'

"No death? Enraptured, my voice trembled believingly.

"'Be patient my child,' said Christ adoring me.

"Touching my head with a loving hand, as a father would his own son, He finished: 'Joy Is A River Ceaselessly Flowing.'

"Floating up, retreating into the cottony perfumed clouds that had gathered above us, I heard Him say finally: 'I will always protect you. Fear not, my beloved, for you have been saved.'

"I stood then alone. Gazing at my hand which had held The Hand of Glory, I saw that it was not a hand that my hand held, but a heart. This miraculous bijou was like a jewel radiating thousands of starry rays in every direction. Overwhelmed, I could feel the unspeakable omnipresence of God, and then I heard the music.

"Shutting my eyes I became disposed to the mellifluous current that swept me away. For a hundred years, or so it seemed to me, this sweet music held me hostage. And when my eyes opened again, once more to gaze upon Christ's beautiful heart, there was Ernst where he had been sitting, playing the violin.

"Returned to the warm fire lit room, I understood that my sojourn into The Other World had come to an end."

Matthew opens his eyes, which are wet with the bitter-sweet dew of his reminiscence. I must admit, I too have been moved by his story. He sips a bit of cognac. So do I.

"Why," I ask, "was Ernst playing the violin?"

"Yes, I wondered the very same thing, and when I asked him he told me that his music made the devil humble. That Satan could not interfere with things as long as he played. To keep me safe, you see."

Matthew's face, denied of expression, is a mysterious mask containing the comportment of secret dignity. Whether or not his story is true, his beatific vision is most certainly true for him, I can see.

"Ernst and I never discussed my experience. Because he already understood what had happened, there was no need for talk.

"Shortly after that, Ernst prepared me safe passage to South America. He foresaw the events that would soon take place in Germany; he delivered me, again, from evil."

"And what became of Ernst?" I ask.

Matthew's withdrawn countenance, quickly arrested by emotion, bespeaks of his sorrow. "Ernst, I had been told, committed suicide not long after my departure," sadly his voice unwraps this personal tragedy. And he looks away from me, attempting for the moment to hide those haunted eyes, eyes haunted not with shame, but with grief. Like him, just then, my grief for David is rediscovered; and silently we sit, two of us, high above the indifferent city, alone.

"Glorious Brazil!" Animated suddenly with pleasure, Matthew startles me with his born-again spirituelle mode.

"It was near Rio de Janeiro that I discovered my new home. Everything had been meticulously arranged by Ernst: passport, money, domicile, a well written menu indeed! I became permanent guest, so to speak, in the home of a very wealthy, very handsome benefactor.

Alexander, was his name. Alexander Epikyklos, a Greek ex-patriot living in Brazil, who had as it were, a friend who was a friend of Ernst.

"Alex, as he came to be known to me, was thirty-nine years old. He owned a very popular dance hall, in Rio, called The Black Orchid. There were of course other business ventures, other interests. His family tree was made of gold, exporting, importing, that sort of thing.

"Like Ernst, Alex's true pleasure was found in the company of young, handsome men. I understood what I was, physically, that is. But I knew also as I grew older, that looks do not necessarily mean everything. Ernst, taught me more than he realized, dear Ernst. As with Ernst, so too with Alex, I became his voluptuous Scheherazade, seducing his mind more than his body."

Listening to Matthew's amazing autobiography has seduced me I think. And thinking that, I can't help to wonder, just then, if this is to be the plot of his great film.

"The rich are a different breed altogether, my dear. And let me tell you something, it makes never mind when in history the rich are rich, they all are a queer lot, they always shall be."

Matthew scans the bright cloudless afternoon sky as though he's looking for objects unidentified. But what I

143

really think is flying through his mind, is another chapter in his roman noir, about to be revealed.

"Alex," Matthew begins again, shooting me with his glass-blue bullet eyes, "was a man of intense passions. He once told me that he was related to Nikos Kazantzakis, the great Greek novelist. Though I can't say whether or not this was true, there is no doubt they shared a very similar vision."

"I see. So what was *his* last temptation?" I question perspicaciously, to let him know, that I know whereof he speaks.

"You are distracting, my dear Nicholas, oh yes you are," Matthew's amused chuckling, a silly cluck, cluck.

"I became very much like a son to Alex. He taught me a great deal, especially about business and finance. I was intimately exposed to his business affairs, and when he saw that I had the knack, as he called it, he installed me legally as his heir.

"And that, my dear Nicky, is how I came to have so much, after being deprived of everything." Matthew softly declares this with a voice of icy triumph.

"Like Ernst," Matthew continues, "Alex died at a young age, but not by his own hand. He had a heart attack, very sudden, with not even the slightest warning. So there I was, twenty-two years old, living in Brazil with wealth beyond my wildest fantasies.

"The war in Europe had ended. Deep, dreadful wounds were healing. I dreamed of returning for a visit, but not to Germany. I have never had the desire to go back there. In my mind it will always be a blood bath, nothing more. So I went on holiday to France.

"Ah, gay Paree! You've been there my boy?"

"Yes, years ago, just a short stay."

"Heavenly! Even war torn, I fell deeply in love with that country. Nicholas, *that* is were I shall make my film. I shall make my film in Paris."

"I almost thought you forgot about your film, Matinee."

"Oh, not at all my dear," Matthew's smile a radiant sunbeam. His teeth are perfect, like Johnny's I think just then. They must be false, is what they must be.

"Nicholas, in France I fell in love with France, but now as an adult, truly for the first time, and in a very different way." Matthew's eyes sparkle suddenly with joy as his charming memory surfaces. This love story preamble makes me crave another shot of booze in which I do indeed indulge.

"Paris, my darling, is like a bejeweled whore," says Matthew boastfully, "and it does not matter whether your preference is for boys or girls, you can't help but to want to make love to her."

"Or perhaps pilfer her jewelry," I inject.

"While on holiday I made the chance acquaintance of a very strange and wonderful woman named Madame Nosostris. Madame Nosostris was, at that time, the famous clairvoyant of Paris. I heard stories about this woman, so with piqued curiosity I paid her a visit, one night, at Cafe Noir on Rue Dragon.

"Rue Dragon twisted up and down, between hidden and quiet old storefronts, like a wet cobblestone serpent. This narrow, ancient little street punctuated this part of Paris like a surreal question mark.

"It was August then, and the weather, which was rainy and sunless, was unusually cold. But for all the right reasons this climate was so becoming to Rue Dragon,

145

highlighting its twisting turns with inky humid shadows that hid from the lamplight.

"At its head, Nicholas, the Dragon was crowned by a tiny subterranean bistro called Cafe Noir, where Madame Nosostris held court.

"Madame Nosostris was a giant woman both in height and girth. Her massive round head was enveloped by an enormous troposphere of raven black hair that was shot through with streaks of white electricity. So pale and delicate was her complexion that even the subtlest wave of sunlight would brutalize. She only ventured out at night.

"Her fleshy face surrounded deep dark brown eyes set wide apart alongside her eagle's beak of a nose. Nonexistent eyebrows were replaced by thinly painted facsimiles; long and black, they were touched by the spider legs of her thickly mascaraed eyelashes.

"Her mouth was a severe red gash, lipstick on lipstick; like a blood red decoupage it hung upon her ghost white face.

"Madame Nosostris, like you darling boy, was Lithuanian, and too, a Jew. She had lived in Paris all of her life and was considered by many to be the wisest woman in Europe. No one could guess her age, precisely because she appeared ageless, and because of her great cerebral prowess, she seemed unearthly."

"She escaped the Nazis?" I ask, wanting to hear more of this story after all.

"She did indeed, my dear. As a matter of fact she *predicted* the Nazis and helped to save many people from their murderous clutches."

"Did your clever clairvoyant own the cafe?"

"Ah, Cafe Noir. So mysterious. No, Cafe Noir was as dark as its name. Its owner, so I was told, was the infamous mistress of a dead Nazi general. The cafe had become a secret stage for many sinister and sometime violent dramas. A backdrop, really, to the affairs of spies and murderers."

"Really, Matinee?"

"Oh, most assuredly, Nicholas. Once, while at the cafe, pretending to be someone other than myself, I saw a murder."

"A murder you say, oh mysterious one?"

"Quite so. A murder most deftly enacted to be sure, Nickypoo. It was done very quickly, and so he thought, surreptitiously, he, that being the murderer you understand, in the Dostoevskian style of Genet: a flashing razor stiletto blade against pale naked neck. Voila! All tension relieved. And I saw it happen, one, two, three."

"More coffee?" Johnny's deep yet hushed voice suddenly disturbs with his sudden reappearance as he tends to the table. As if by habit, he delicately fusses with the flower arrangement, bothering the already perfect centerpiece like a bored old grandmother.

"Nicholas, more coffee?" Matthew dashes me with a questioning glance, as I reach for my pack of Salems, putting one to mouth.

"No thank you dear one, but another splash of this *wunderbar* liquid might just do the trick," I say as I bring flame to fag. Into my glass Johnny pours the light fantastic. "*Danke*, handsome," I respond, smiling up at the much too handsome face.

With service complete, Johnny vanishes.

147

"Now, where was I?" Matthew asks, knowing I'm sure, exactly where he was.

"La murderette." Providing the answer, I adjust myself in my chair.

"Quite honestly Nicholas, I think that the murderer was a transvestite."

"*Tres* macabre. What makes you think so?"

"Something in the way she moved me. When I looked at her: her hairdo, the makeup, her *arms*. Yes-- yes that's it! Her arms were much too-- too muscled."

"Well love, what would a nice muscular transvestite like her be doing in a place like that?"

"She was tense, dearest. She needed to relieve tension. With a drink or two, I suppose, and then a murder. Anyway, I am sure that she was a spy. Lots of that was going on in those days you know."

"No, actually, I hadn't."

"Well none the less it was. Most probably a spy, Miss Incognita, snooping for secrets, came upon her long awaited victim."

"Fate is kind,
She brings to those who love,
The sweet fulfillment of,
Their secret longing."

I sing this to the tune of *When You wish Upon A Star*. Matthew does not look impressed. I can't imagine why.

"Anyway, God only knows what really happened, but I'll never in my life forget the look on that sailor's face as that blade sliced his throat from ear to ear."

I am chilled for a second as I think of Genet's *Querelle*. And I wonder just then, if I am better off for the opportunity of only having read about such things?

"Anyway, Nicholas, it was that very same strange evening that I met Madame Nosostris. I had been at the cafe twice before, hoping that our paths would cross. And like those very permanent astral constellations, woven starry arabesques, whose paths cross from ancient time to ancient time, ours did indeed intersect that night."

"Come to the cabaret old chum!" I smile.

"Madame Nosostris had a bad cold. She sipped from a yellow china cup an elixir of steaming blueberry tea with brandy. Her moon size eyes played over the spread of Tarot cards before her. She had a bad cold, you understand, but her gift of sight, as she called it, was unfailing.

"I sat at the table before her. I was her chosen guest. A young Persian waiter, a beautiful Iranian boy with a dull glass eye, served me wine. Madame Nosostris brought her tea cup to her mouth and sipped the hot liquid. Steam, rising from the cup, touched her eyes making the lids flutter like great lavender moths. *'Le coeur a ses raisons que la raison ne connait point,'* she sang the words, sotto voce, as the yellow cup was returned to the table beside her magic cards. Wet lipstick stained the rim of the china cup leaving an impression of her kiss."

"Translate, *s'il vous plaît*."

"She said: The heart has its reasons that reason knows nothing of. I had no idea what she meant, at least not then."

"The wisdom of the heart," I whisper.

"The woman told me that I was different-- someone not of this world, someone very much like her.

She spoke of the Hanged Man, one of her cards I surmised, and of death.

"Her tumid eyes could be seen moving back and forth beneath violet pink lids as she spoke. Coal black spider leg eyelashes appeared embraced as if to hold the magnolia blossom lids shut. She said that the Tarot cards brought color to her eyes, but it was the spirits of the dead who whispered in her ear.

"Madame Nosostris said I was no stranger to death's company-- that I was known quite well by many of these spirits who came to speak to her.

"She told me I had been touched directly by God, and like her, I had seen His Son.

"'You shall meet a woman,' Madame Nosostris proclaimed, 'and she shall become the vessel of your true happiness.'"

"Good god, Matinee! For a minute there you almost had me convinced."

"But it is true, Nicholas, I did meet a woman. And she, *alava sholom*, gave me that which is my greatest achievement-- my nepenthe. My son Johnny."

"Johnny!" I'm shocked, truly I am. Matinee's mind-boggling sonata has absolutely boggled my mind. "But Matthew, I-- I thought--"

"Dearest, I know you did, and that is why I always played along. It was a fun little game, don't you think? You know child, an old man needs some fun sometime too."

Matthew's gay little story (gay, that is, in the old way) has got me by the balls. All I can do now is listen. And suddenly it comes back to me. His weird little trick of word play about Miss Shirley Understood and Mister Herr! I've been had, I think.

"When I returned to Brazil, not long after my Parisian holiday, I was introduced to a most delicious South American creature, by her somewhat ignoble parents.

"They were basically good people enough, I must admit, who had as it were, invested everything that they owned into the *making* of this woman child of theirs. You must understand, this sort of thing was, and still is, a very common practice among the, oh, how shall I put it, the lower-middle class in those there regions. *Si, si?*" Matthew smiles rapaciously. I simply nod incredulously.

"Her name was Desiree Desifinado," continues Matthew, licking his chops like some kind of plebeian hetero football jock. "And she was drenchingly lovely. A deliriously attractive girl. So witty. So smart. So chic! Ours was a most mysterious affair."

"I bet!" I spit.

"Desiree, with my heart, held me prisoner."

And evidently with another organ of a decidedly somewhat more personal nature, I think.

"Madame Nosostris *knew* you see. Desiree seduced me, Nicholas, in truly a most unexpected and unique way. Unique, that is, in that I had never before been with *la femme.*"

"Oh, *chercher la femme, mon amie!*"

"You may scoff, Nicholas, but rest assured Desiree Desifinado's love, for me, was something other than earthly."

"You married her?"

"We were married, yes. And for the interim of her short life-- it is true Nicholas that I am not a stranger to death's company, I gave my wife every conceivable comfort and happiness. In turn, Desiree, my sweet lovely girl, gave me Johnny. She died, and I am most unhappy to report, in child birth."

Matthew withdraws again suddenly into a tranquilized silence and stillness. A sort of senescent autism has grabbed him it seems.

The sun, obscured by dark joyless clouds has been put out momentarily. Rain, in a quick unexpected drizzle, pisses on us. Gusts of wind shatteringly invade our quiet private afternoon chat, pulling flowers out of the vase on the table, that Matthew's *son* had so carefully arranged.

I do not, all of a sudden, feel well. And as I think this, with animal instinct, I run from my chair and head to the can to puke.

♟

"Are you alright, Nicholas?" Matthew questions from his great wicker king's chair as I make my reappearance in the living room. "You gave me a bit of a fright out there, leaping and dashing, without a moments notice." The old man observes me like the Mother Prioress. His eyes have acquired the darkness of unpolished silver. They match my new mood.

"I'm fine Matthew, really. Nothing a brisk walk won't cure."

"Well then, I suspect that you wish to be getting along. But Nicholas, I do have a task for you, as I am sure you may have gathered. I need you to find me another young man. You are so good at this, you know. Quite the casting agent you turned out to be." Matthew displays a fugitive smile.

"What do you have a taste for this time, dear one?" I ask. "White meat or dark?" I just want to tell the old lady to fuck off, but it's the money I want.

Matthew licks his upper lip with the tip of his pink tongue.

"Actually, my stunning blond Baltic beauty, it's of *you* I have always dreamed, but fortunately tastes do change. I'd like something a bit younger, fresher. You do know what I mean, don't you Nicky?"

It's a double-edged insult he's cut me with, the old fuck! I'll send him to the hospital in a minute. I smile with the understanding that old queens never lie, they just lose their friends.

"So, it's a fluffy white chicken you're after, huh Father Feelemup? Correctol?"

"That is correct." And the old man rises from his bamboo throne like a reedy withered emperor.

"Here," Matthew hands me the familiar ivory colored envelope, "is your fee. It's more than usual, because this time this boy must be very special. You see, Nicholas, I haven't--" the aged voice cracks involuntarily, as the eyes turn off for a moment, "I haven't the energy for this sort of thing anymore, and I want this one to be so very special."

He's hiding something I can tell. He stinks of secrets. And I think that's pure shit. My compassion is dwindling fast.

"Nicholas, I want him to have green, green eyes. This boy must have eyes smaragdine as emeralds. Do you understand me?" His question almost a frightened, breathless plea. "I want this beautiful blond angel to have strange, beautiful eyes. Eyes that shall bewitch me I

153

pray!" Matthew lets himself drop, again on his throne, dissipated.

"Don't worry Matthew," I say as I show myself to the door to leave. I know exactly what to do. "I can see those strange, angelic eyes, now."

19

∞

I am walking down State Street, when I spot a friend of mine. His name is Hugo. Hugo is his last name but he uses it as a first. This Hugo is a short Oriental Mexican with over developed muscles that he got at the gym pumping iron and steroids. He's one of those fags who spends almost every free moment he has killing himself in the weight room, so that the tricks he picks up can kill themselves on his biceps.

I met Hugo one night in a leather bar on Clark Street, not too far from where we are now about to meet. The friend I was with that night, at that bar, said, 'See that *too* fuckin' hot leather boy over there? That's Hugo. He has the dick of death.'

"Hey, Nick, good to see you man. *Que pa sa?*" Hugo says with a giant salsa and chop suey grin. His perpetually tan face is hairless. A long thin knife scar cuts boastfully across his high right cheekbone. The scar makes him look even more beautiful than he is already.

"Good to see you, Hugo. It's been a while. Where you off to?"

"I'm goin' for a couple beers at the Redoubt," Hugo tells me, and then asks me to join him, that he'll buy me one. How can I resist? Besides, Hugo's quite a riot not to mention one hot piece of ass. He smells of sex. And his cock, John Thursday Hugo affectionately calls it, always looks hard and ready in his pants, which I'm sure it is.

Good old Hugo. He's one of those guys, that even other straight guys, secretly turn their eyes to steal a look at. I know that Hugo has had one or two of them at least. He says he's had a cop, *straight city*, in the alley right in back of the cop's girlfriend's apartment. He said he sucked the cop's dick, right there, before he was going in to fuck her. Hugo says that the cop gave John Thursday the third degree too. Jesus, what will they think of next?

"So, where you comin' from?" Hugo inquires. His question brings back memories of the afternoon that I was trying to forget.

Remember to remember. Strange eyes.

Too bad Hugo didn't have a thing for old men. Matinee would cum just smelling this stud's jock strap.

"Visiting my poor, decrepit aunt in the old folks home," I let Hugo know. It's much better than the truth I think. But then, it really is the truth.

"Too bad. Is she very sick?" Hugo asks.

"Sick is not the word," I say as we turn to enter the bar.

Inside, the bar is dark, and my eyes take a while to adjust to the dimly lit interior. The air, heavy and stale, smells of smoke and piss. This place has never been one of my favorite joints. I can't, or perhaps I can, imagine what Hugo finds so fascinating about this place. It's a shitty little hole in the wall with roaches and mice and sullen fags in leather drag who, like Dracula, hate the light. I once spit a fly out of my mouth with a mouthful of beer in this dump. Today I'll take it in the bottle-- the beer, not the fly.

156

We take our seats at the end of the long rectangular bar. "What'll ya have, boys?" the weasely little bespectacled bartender asks us with a damp Australian drawl.

We both order the same thing: Miller in the bottle. The bartender turns to get the beer, and I notice he's wearing a black leather vest with matching leather pants, and there are holes cut out in the back of these pants to let his ass stick through. How charming I think, as I catch a look at this tiny uninspiring hairy ass. What a sight! 'Peekaboo,' his assette says, 'I see you.' Aussie should think again before donning this ensemble. Better yet, he should let Hugo show him how it's done.

Hugo tells me, as we drink our beer, as I light my one remaining Salem, that he's been preparing, night and day, for the Mr. Gay Chicago Contest. Working out *eight* days a week has never made his body better, I can see. How can he not win this most coveted title, I wonder, as my eyes wander over every wave and crest, nook and cranny, Dick and Jane, of his more than ample physique. Stunning, sister! Yes, it is most definitely a body to behold, this Hugo has. It is-- there can be no question-- not a one could doubt, that this is the true Body of God that was most obviously meant to be eaten.

I ask Hugo about his love life. It's really his sex life I mean. From what I know about Hugo, there is very little love, if any at all, in his life. It's always this trick or that trick with Hugo, never a lover or even a boyfriend. 'Marriage is a prison,' he sighs. I'm glad to see he's still alive; he's never looked better. But Hugo assures me that his sex is as safe as can be. *Oolala*! Up the old arse with a rubbered hose. And we all know that as long as he doesn't cum in your mouth it's simply sunshine. 'I'm not giving *It* up under any circumstances. I'd *rather* die!' he proclaims quite heroically.

Funny, Hugo tells me that he doesn't even know anybody, personally that is, who has it, or who has died of it. What a comedian this Hugo is. He makes me laugh until I want to cry.

I tell Hugo that I have to take a piss, so I finish my beer and head for the john. He says a cold one will be waiting, with a shot, when I get back.

"J.D., Nick?"

"What else?"

⚱

There are two johns in this bar. But then, there are at least two johns in every queer joint. One is for Ladies, the other, for Ladies. What difference does it make anyway, we all have the same plumbing, when you get right down to it.

One can is occupied, so I go to the other door marked MEN.

The door slams behind me, pulled back into place by a tight rusting spring. I secure the door shut with its hook lock. I am surprised to find one there at all.

This is one act I want to do alone, particularly in this shit hole. And what a shit hole it is! From the smell of things, I have to breathe through my mouth or I know I'd puke, and puking once a day is enough. Just thinking of the stink that is floating into my open mouth, as I pull my prick out to piss, almost makes me gag. But the hot pleasure of the release of my piss from my swelling bladder helps me not to, until my eyes meet the large turd which is floating in the urinal into which my piss doth flow. Oh Happy Day! The turd winks at me as I give it a golden shower. And as I pull my eyes up from this exalted sight, of what can only be construed as one man's inhumanity to another, I see The Word, divinely scrawled in bright red lipstick on the wall above my head: IN THE BEGINNING GOD CREATED FAIRIES AND THEY MADE MEN. Truly, I think to myself, I have been saved.

⇧

As I pass by the jukebox, Patsy Cline, God bless her broken heart, starts singing *Sweet Dreams*. Some seven foot tall leather queen is throwing a few spare quarters into the juke. This guy looks like Lurch from the Adams Family I think, as I get a close-up of his puss. And he's all dreamy eyed too, Lurch is. Swaying his hips oh so delicately to the music; his lips, wet with the beer he's swilling and the sweet wet dreams he's dreaming, move gently in silent imitation of Miss Cline's lamentation. Perhaps Lurch thinks he *is* Patsy. Or better yet, he's Jessica Lange playing Patsy in the movie. That's it! Oh, k. d. lang, where are you when we need you?

Lurch's quarters have reminded me that it's Salem time. So I go to where the flavor is, and deposit the absurdly large amount of money needed, into the machine.

I turn and see Hugo talking with some young kid at the bar. His hand is rubbing the boy's crotch. The kid is just his type; they look like each other. And I can see too, that they are both quite content in their gay conversation. Happy even. All ear to ear grins, a beautiful transparent paper that perpetually gift wraps ever empty chit chat. New yet used smiles, selfishly and powerfully given to each other, to keep others at bay. And this is why I am aware, without asking, that they do not know each other, that they have just met.

They are performing an ancient ritual. It is a prelude to what the night has in store for them. Soon it will be into the night life for Hugo and his young admirer. Another trick for Hugo. They are about to begin the beguine. I can do without the shot and the cold one.

⚱

Outside of the bar the approaching night again had acquired its winter personality. Wind-gusts, with the sense of humor of icy steel, treaded heavily against evening walkers. Street lamps coming on vibrated with blue translucent halos, each one, a tiny moon, floated above the street. The moon, full and silver, above the lamps, slowly rose higher into the twilight sky.

But there are other kinds of twilight. Twilight not just of an evening sky and not just of the Gods. There is the twilight of the human mind; a vacant place made known by strange and unfathomable twists of life. The now you see it, the now you don't. The here today, the gone tomorrow. It is the unmistakable fingerprint of Fate, that gal we all know and love.

On this night, Force Majeure had lost a dear friend. Sam, the bartender, Nicholas's good friend, had died. Just as Nicholas stepped out of the bar into the street, and lit a cigarette, Sam died. Nicholas breathed in the smoke; Sam breathed his last breath. At that moment the smoke from his cigarette burned his throat. He choked as the cold mentholated smoke invaded his lungs. Sam died and the ventilator tube was extracted from his throat. He died in the drug induced twilight of morphine, his artificial, mechanically sustained life, ended.

There are other kinds of twilight. The Gods may offer only so much. But then, after all, they are only just Gods.

20

∞

"Sam would have been thirty years old this April," Sam's mother gently speaks these words again, for what seems like a thousand times, but now as if it were only the first, to Nicholas. The woman's eyes, swollen and red, irritated that way from crying, filled once more with tears. They both stood there, before Sam in his casket, the casket surrounded abundantly with floral remembrances.

Nicholas delicately holds the mother's hands in his, the way people do at times like that, as if this were his own mother; though strangers, they stood side by side holding their hands in that intimate embrace, silently communicating to each other a profound, unspeakable sympathy.

It was early in the evening, but many people, friends and relatives that had come to see Sam and pay their respects to his parents, had already begun to gather in that long room of the funeral chapel.

An elderly man, with a rough red Irish face, who sat alone on the sofa before the casket, Nicholas recognized to be Sam's father. He had met the man, only once, several years ago. They had had a few boilermakers, Sam and his father and Nicholas. They had shared a few laughs too. And the time that had gone by, since that time, had not changed the man much, except that he had lost most of his hair Nicholas noticed.

The father appeared sullen, a look of contempt and loss draped his hard face. This was a man who had probably seen it all, from the back side of things that is: a war or two, poverty, alcoholism, divorce from his wife, the death of parents, of brothers and sisters, of friends, and of his faith in God and the Church. But tonight this man was attempting to come to grips with subject matter far more arresting. His only son, he had just found out during his son's only illness, was a faggot. And this son had died quite abruptly and very horribly of a faggot's shameful, incurable disease.

Perhaps, the man thought, that his act of turning away from God, that turning his back on the *One Holy Apostolic Catholic Church*, had brought death to his son.

But no, how could that be thought the man again? He raised his eyes up, only for them to come to rest upon the face of Christ, a face which rested so serenely upon the silver cross that had been placed in his son's casket. He remembered just then a verse from the bible. Something he had heard so very long ago. One thing that had moved him, a new father, so very much: *For God so loved the world that he gave his only begotten son--*. No, Sam's father thought; God, even if he did betray him with apathy, could never have done this to his only begotten.

It was Sam, the man thought again, who had brought this tragedy upon himself, killing himself, and marking his family with stigma.

"You know," Sam's mother said to Nicholas breaking their silence, "Sam would have graduated from the university this year too."

163

The woman, devastated by the ever shifting facets of what-might-have-been-if-only, choked into sobs and moved closer to the casket, to look more closely at her boy.

Kneeling before the casket the woman trembled with grief. Her hands, like small gray sparrows, moved this way and that way on her son's arm with delicate brevity, as if not to hurt him.

Nicholas looked at Sam again, his eyes drawn to the young man's face. He had seen this face before and not only with David. This was the face of the too young to die, the Halloween face that only dimly resembled reality. And once more, as so often the case, because of someone's thoughtful concern, a large framed photograph of the dead stood upon a small table near the casket, beautifully providing evidence of what was once quite beautiful and very much alive.

Nicholas turned away from Sam's resting place. He's better off, Nicholas thought. Better off than to have lingered on like David, in and out of the hospital, until every distinguishable characteristic of life had ceased to be distinguished. At least he went fast. Less than four weeks. He's better off, Nicholas thought again.

"Mr. Homan," Nicholas said to Sam's father as he approached him, as the man stood to acknowledge him and shake his hand, "I am so deeply sorry."

Taking the older man's hand into his, Nicholas's eyes filled with tears. He saw, as he looked at the man, not Sam's father, but his own. It had not been a long time since Nicholas had thought about his father, that time being in Gabriel's bedroom the night it rained, but it seemed like forever to Nicholas since he last imagined what his father

164

looked like. Yet, this man standing before him, looked nothing at all like his father who was long since dead. What Nicholas did see though, as he gazed upon the haunted empty face, was the face of all fathers grieving for their children who have gone before them.

"Thank you young man," Mr. Homan responded, politely ending the handshake. Nicholas pinched the bridge of his nose between his eyes to stop the tears.

"I remember you," Mr. Homan said, "but, I'm sorry, I have forgotten your name."

"Nicholas, sir. Nicholas Staskis. Sam and I were friends. We stopped by to see you once, a few years ago. We drank boiler--" his voice cracked, "makers. We had a good time, I remember." Nicholas looked down attempting not to cry.

"Yes," Mr. Homan said with a smile in his voice, "I remember that. We did have a good time, didn't we."

More people had come to see Sam, and the room filled.

The perfume of flowers in the warm room was heavy, and now and then, among silence and the hushed exchange of words, crying could be heard from women and men.

And Nicholas's heart, again quite broken, went out to Sam's mother who was shattered and always would be, and to Sam's father who tried not to appear so, but was.

⇧

Nicholas looks around the crowded room after Sam's father excuses himself. He sees familiar faces. Many of these people, mostly young men, are regulars of Force Majeure where Sam tended bar. And, as Nicholas takes

165

inventory of these many solemn faces, he sees Gary, the owner of Force Majeure, and Justine, the cocktail server, enter the room.

Nicholas observes them move slowly together toward the casket, their arms are entwined formally. Gary wears a black double breasted suit, his face is drawn profoundly serious. These events are nothing new to Gary. They have become now as commonplace as cocktail parties.

Justine, in mourning, appears perfected in graciousness. Death seems to bring to her life a new meaning, a new look. She no longer betrays herself with a camp, burlesque transvestitism, but has, it appears, suddenly metamorphosed into that which she hopes she truly is: A Lady.

The tall, provocative Justine too, is gilt in black. Her lightly made-up face is covered by a veil, as though a spider has woven a web from her angled hat to the tip of her chin. Her ebony hair, neatly coifed in a French twist, is pulled back away from her face, and sparkling on each ear is a tiny diamond. Mourning becomes Justine, Nicholas thinks, as he watches the couple respectfully kneel before Sam's casket and pray.

Death, thinks Nicholas, as he considers this scene, is a most obscene choreographer, infusing reality into illusion and confusing illusion with life.

This must all be a dream, Nicholas thinks to himself, as his mind soars back to the moment when he first sees David in his casket: *this cannot be real*.

And the overwhelming feeling of suddenly fainting passes as he regards Gary and Justine in his presence.

⇧

"You don't look so good, hon," Justine said to Nicholas as she took his arm. Guiding him to a chair, the threesome sat.

Gary's eyes, glazed with grief, sparkled softly. Obvious to Nicholas, the man had been crying. Even cowboys cry, Nicholas thought, as he pulled himself together. Gary, the big Texas cowboy, looked like a little boy who had been slapped very hard. Composed, as best as he was, Gary looked as though he was about to come unwrapped at any moment.

Justine, however, came across like the Dowager Mother, perfect calm, blissfully in control.

She's on drugs, Nicholas thought, as he half listened to Justine's strangely modulated voice deliver, what he thought to be, a pathetically naive sermonette on death and dying and life and living. She was speaking about The Rapture, and Heavenly Light, and Christ's Great Heart-O-Love, when he saw the angel, Gabriel, kneel before Sam's casket.

"I don't believe it," Nicholas whispered, "it is a small world."

Gabriel studied Sam's face and hair. It's all wrong, he thought. The hair is all wrong. Sam didn't wear his hair like this. Gabriel touched the hair on Sam's forehead and brushed it up, quickly, with his fingertips. Sam would have killed me if I ever styled his hair like this, thought Gabriel.

They should have had me do it. I've done it for more than a year now; they should have known better.

Oh, Sam, you were such a beautiful and good person. How can you be dead? How can this awful thing keep happening to such wonderful people?

Remembering his friend, Gabriel's tears, like unexpected rain, ran down his face. He wiped his face with a handkerchief, then buried the wet cloth in his suit coat pocket as he stood.

Gabriel moved to the tiny woman, who standing nearby, but not alone, he knew to be Sam's mother. She had been an occasional client, preferring to do her hair herself. But for special occasions, a party, a wedding, she had gone to Gabriel and he had made her, '*lovely,*' as she would remark while admiring herself in the mirror.

This was not a special occasion, Gabriel thought, as he approached the wilted woman. She had not even touched her hair. She looked so very pitiful.

"I'm so sorry, Mrs. Homan. I'm so terribly sorry," Gabriel offered as he lovingly took the little woman into his arms.

They both cried again, as they would again, before parting, before the night there ended. And as they shared their grief, locked closely together in their numb embrace, Nicholas observed them. And he felt as he joined them, though distantly in this way from his seat, that he was in love with the angel Gabriel. But he demanded this not of himself, cutting this feeling away, like amputation.

Strange eyes. Eyes smaragdine as emeralds. Paris green eyes.

And then Mrs. Homan and Gabriel parted. Turning away from the woman, Gabriel's eyes fell upon Nicholas and their glances touched.

"What's the matta, shuga?" Justine whispered to Nicholas theatrically low. "Looks like you just seen some ghost." Justine turned to look in the direction of Nicholas's stare. "That ain't no ghost, hon," she said, and looking back at Nicholas continued, "Dat be dat pretty boy you was sittin' with da otha night. He musta knowd Sam. He sure do look pretty in dat suit of his, huh shuga?"

Without a word, Nicholas stood and moved toward Gabriel. Gabriel maneuvered through the crowd in the front of the room and moved toward Nicholas.

"I guess the play's off," Gabriel said to Nicholas, his spurious smile fading.

Nicholas said, "The play?"

"Yes, we were going to go. You forgot, I understand. Don't worry."

"Of course, *The Glamour of Evil*. No, I really didn't forget, but you're right, it's definitely off. How are you?"

"Alright, except for this."

"Yes, this." Nicholas closed his eyes for a moment, then opened them again, into Gabriel's.

"How did you know him?" Nicholas asked.

"We were friends. I cut his hair," Gabriel said.

"That's it?" Nicholas questioned in a tone that Gabriel immediately understood. He hoped that friendship is all that there was to their relationship; however, he did not understand why he felt that way. Not just then.

"Yes, Nicholas. Really, we were just friends," Gabriel answered truthfully. "And you?" Gabriel hoped for the same answer, and he did understand why.

"Friends. For years. We met in San Francisco, when I lived there, and he lived there for a time. He moved back to Chicago long before I did. I - never - intended - to - move - here - though," Nicholas said as an aside, his voice fading as his thoughts wandered a bit.

"I'm glad you did," Gabriel said. And he smiled, and this time his smile was very real.

Nicholas smiled and said, "Would you like to go with me to the lobby for some coffee? I really need a cigarette."

"Sure, let's go," said Gabriel.

As they moved together through the crowded room and out the door, the young Irish priest who had arrived, invited those assembled there to pray.

21

∞

They sat in two giant leather upholstered chairs, Nicholas and Gabriel, as far away as they could from others, in the large bright lobby of the funeral chapel. Each held a styrofoam cup filled with coffee. Nicholas smoked, Gabriel declined the invitation, insisting that he was quitting.

"Did you know that Sam was in the hospital the night we met?" Nicholas asked Gabriel.

"Yes, I did. I knew a couple of days before. He was in twice in six weeks. I can't believe it. He died so suddenly."

"I just heard that night that he was in again with pneumonia. It's all so horrible."

"You know," Gabriel said, "what I told you about my father, Sebastian?"

Nicholas nodded.

"He died of AIDS. But I didn't tell you that, did I?"

"No, you didn't, but I knew. You didn't have to tell me, I just knew. Anyway, Oona and I had a little heart-to-heart over coffee before I left your apartment. She told me everything. Her coffee was definitely better than this." Nicholas winked.

"Yeah, she likes it strong," Gabriel laughed. "You're not upset with me, about my father, I mean?" Gabriel asked.

"Why should I be?" asked Nicholas.

"The AIDS thing you know," said Gabriel.

"Gabriel, let me share something with you. I almost never talk about this, you understand, because it's just too painful for me. I had a lover for seven years. I hate that word: lover. Anyway, David and I-- his name was David, we were together for seven truly wonderful years, and then he died of AIDS. Poof, all gone. Just like that. Snap! and it was all over. How do you like that? No. Why on earth would I be upset with you?"

"I'm sorry Nicholas-- I mean, about David. That's horrible," Gabriel said and his eyes became wet.

"I will kill you if you start crying, Gabriel. I just got over the feeling," Nicholas said half joking. Looking away from him he sipped his coffee.

"Are you alright though-- I mean, well you know?"

Gabriel realized suddenly that he was trespassing on very private property. His face flushed red and he stopped his question and looked down.

"Have I got it you mean?" Nicholas asked focusing his eyes again on the angel.

"Yes," Gabriel said not looking up, trying to conceal his embarrassment.

"No. As far as every doctor, witch and otherwise I've been to can tell, I am negative. Hip hooray!" Nicholas laughed dryly. "Anyway, and will you please look at me."

Gabriel lifted his face.

"Anyone who is interested in anyone has the right to know these things. So please *Louise*, don't fret, it wasn't a faux pas," Nicholas said.

Gabriel smiled not knowing what to say next.

"What about you?" Nicholas asked.

"Negative. I've had all the tests, over and again. My bill of health, as they say, is clean," Gabriel said relaxing and sat back.

"That's good," Nicholas said. And he became silent for a moment. Thoughts stirred quickly in his mind, and then he continued, "I have an old friend who I would like you to meet, Gabriel. I think the two of you would hit it off. He's a filmmaker, quite good really, and, well, in some circles, well-known. Anyway he's in terrible need of a new hairstylist. His hair looks like Andy Warhol's."

"That's a shame," Gabriel said, somewhat confused by the odd turn of the conversation.

"Yes, really. Anyway he's quite wealthy and all of that. He owns at Marina City, but he lives all over the world. I think you could really help him out this way, and I know that he could help you too, financially, I mean. What do you think?"

"Fine," Gabriel said, "when?"

"I'll tell you what," Nicholas said smiling, "I've got your number. I'll call you soon and arrange an appointment. I know any time would be good for Matthew, my old friend, that is."

With that, Nicholas stood, and walked to the entrance of the funeral chapel, and left.

22

∞

I cannot sleep and it is so late. Is it because it is so late that I cannot sleep, or can I not sleep because it is so late? Ah, who the fuck knows I think. I am desperate for deep dreamless sleep, but I cannot sleep, and my only comfort, my Savior, my hope, is this liquor, this booze.

"Pour me another, doll," I say out loud to myself. I just spill a drop. "Oh, just a little *dropeepoo*." This'll knock me out I hope. Should have saved those ludes; now would've been *the* time, you bettcha.

The living room is dark. Sam's face will not leave me. The angel's eyes keep their watch over me. I am tormented by the smell of roses, but there are no flowers here.

"*Flores para los muertos*," I am laughing. I am profoundly drunk. I remind myself of Richard Burton in *Who's Afraid of Virginia Woolf,* but I feel like Taylor: "Who's afraid of Virginia Woolf? Virginia Woolf, Virginia Woolf. Who's afraid--. I am George. I am." I can't stop laughing. "Poor, Nicholas. Sad. Sad." I'm laughing so hard I think I might laugh myself to death.

The room is cold. I should've made a fire. I can't stop laughing.

I *want* to laugh myself to death!

I can see the clock in the kitchen. It's two in the old morning.

Jesus H. I need to sleep. But every time I lie down on this fucking sofa I feel like I'm drowning. I can't shut my eyes. When I shut my eyes I see ghosts and angels and vampires. But they aren't the ghosts and angels and vampires I want to see.

"God, Sam! You told me you believed in life after death. Can't you see me then, you asshole? Can't you see just how fucking miserable I am? So where the hell are you, Sam? Why can't you, and that other cocksucker, David, make a guest appearance? I - AM - WAITING!"

🏛

"Nicholas, is that you? What's wrong?" Gabriel answers the phone half-awake. The red numbers on his clock glow 3:00.

"I'm sorry. I-- I shouldn't of called. So. So. Late," Nicholas responds slowly, drunkenly. He has been crying, and his voice is raspy.

"No, it's ok, really. Talk to me, I'm here. Do you want me to come where you are?" Gabriel asks, his heart beating hard and fast as he sits down on the mattress.

"I-- I don't know what I want, Gabriel," Nicholas says. "No, I do know what I want. I want to sleep. Sleep. But - I - can't. At all."

Gabriel remains quiet. Listening.

Nicholas begins to cry again. Sobbing into the phone, he presses it against his chin. "I want to know where God is." Through clenched teeth he says beseechingly: "WHERE IS GOD?"

Silence.

Very calmly, with a calculated knowing certainty, Gabriel answers: "He's out on the back porch, sleeping with the cat, Nicholas."

Suddenly, Nicholas begins laughing very hard, as he sees in his drunken mind's eye, God the dog, asleep on the back porch. But this time it is healing laughter, a catharsis, just the thing he needs.

After his laughter subsides, he says to Gabriel, "I want to be with you tomorrow, if that sounds alright. I'm not going to the funeral. I just can't," he says and begins to feel a bit sober. Tired now, with the feeling to sleep, his body grows heavy.

"I'm going," Gabriel says, "I need to, but it's in the morning, and you'll probably sleep late anyway. I'll meet you afterward, ok, Nicholas?"

"Yes. Fine. Afterward."

"We can meet for lunch," Gabriel suggests.

"Ok," Nicholas agrees.

"Where?" Gabriel asks.

"How about Jerome's?" Nicholas offers. "Very pleasant. You know where it is?" he asks.

"Yes, I do. That sounds good, Nicholas. I'll meet you, around one. Wait for me if I'm not there on the dot, ok? Get some sleep."

"I will, now, I think."

"Good night, Nicholas."

"Night, Gabriel."

Sweet angel, good night.

23

∞

Nicholas sat by himself at the bar at Jerome's. While waiting for Gabriel he drank a Bloody Mary. The hangover he was nursing was beginning to respond quite nicely to treatment. A lovely chemotherapy, he thought. Lighting a Salem he put it to his lips. *Salem: it means peace.* He remembered Gabriel's words.

Looking around the calmly illuminated large room, he saw it, as if for the first time. The very atmosphere, light and airy, appeared variegated with shades of green and beige. Enormous potted palms, which had been arranged among draped tables and elegant columns, seduced him. Palm court music played discreetly in the background. He recognized the piece, a tango: *La Cumparsita.*

"The tango," Nicholas whispered out loud to no one.

David loved this music he thought. The ambiance the music painted went well with his mood. It was strangely dark, yet uplifting, and it took his thoughts back to a not so distant time of great happiness. David understood this music, Nicholas thought as he listened to its handsome boldness. And David understood the dance.

But then, he had to, because he was nothing less than a champion. Ballroom competition dancing was David's life, next to him, of course.

David was incredible, Nicholas smiled in recollection, as a stream of living memories suddenly flooded his mind. Like light, imported all at once into a space of pitch blackness, Nicholas's shuttered consciousness cleared. He began to remember things, that until just then, had been deeply hidden within him. His emotional suffocation was ending.

David, and his partner Karen, had danced together since childhood. They, like brother and sister, devoted, and perhaps even more so because both were only-children, seemed seamless.

'We will always be together, Karen, because we will always love each other,' little David had once promised her.

But Karen, as she grew older, into that time when simple and innocent fondness between playmates may gradually transform into the complex emotional gift of love, which could be shared between bedmates, began to realize that something was decidedly different about her and David's relationship.

He loved her, yes, this she understood without doubt. But his love for her was too gentle, too kind. He seldom touched her, except for when they danced. And even when they danced, and the dance was intensely sensual, his touch always professional, was regulated with an artistic passion, never the passion of sexuality. He *was* decidedly different, she knew.

Karen, a well read, well traveled young lady, one hardly naive, who had had abundant acquaintanceships with many a colorful character, began to suspect the truth about the young man whom she loved. And the truth was, as most truths are, painful in its simplicity: her handsome, masculine, rakish young man had an eye for other handsome, masculine, rakish young men. What could she do? *Nada*. So she adjusted; she got over it, as they who are gay say.

Then one day, once upon a time, David met Nicholas. And as all good fairytales do have, a happy ending to this *menage a trois* was right around the corner. The boys became lovers, and the girl remained near and dear, right up to the tragic last moment.

But the happy ending ended.

Karen gave the eulogy at David's funeral and almost died that day. Soon after she took her seat, and as she would say later, from the most excruciating ordeal of her life, she suffered a somewhat more major than minor stroke. It was the result of an aneurysm to be precise, which ended her dancing days forever.

Bravely and silently Karen made it through, till the funeral pyre was lit, and then she collapsed into unconsciousness, narrowly missing the threshold of Death's Door by less than is measurable.

The surgeon proclaimed it a miracle; her mother knew better: God's will. Nonetheless, Karen's best friend became her electric wheelchair, which by grace of the ever miraculous will of God, she has sat in pathetically, partially paralyzed, ever since.

And Nicholas thought, as he remembered all of this, that he needed to give Karen a call, it had been far too long since the last one.

He looked at his watch and he saw that it was almost one-thirty. It didn't matter to him that Gabriel had not yet arrived. Funerals, such that they were, always involved unexpected time. Anyway, he was beginning to enjoy himself. In a strange way his enjoyment began to matter to him. He was looking forward to this date, with the angel. He no longer felt any guilt.

And as his mind became suddenly free to accept again the experience of this kind of enjoyment guiltlessly, he knew that his decision not to go to Sam's funeral was correct. Let the dead be with the dead he thought. He felt like living.

David, for too long a time had monopolized his mind, desperately possessing him even more so in death. Anais, Nicholas knew, had not been wrong when she hauled him over the coals about his behavior. But, what Anais did not understand, what she could not see clearly enough, is that an exorcism was in order. The shaman had to be called in. The Angel of Mercy invoked. But then, just perhaps, they had been. The Gods help those to help themselves to those who can help.

"Sorry I'm late, Nicholas," Gabriel's voice arose with a soft abruptness from behind Nicholas. Gabriel took a seat at the bar next to him.

"You're not late, Gabriel," Nicholas smiled, really feeling happy to see him. "You cannot be late from a funeral, unless of course you're the corpse. Then you would be the late Gabriel, which you are not." They both laughed. "Would you like a vodka gimlet?" Nicholas asked.

"You remembered my drink. Sure, I think a double is what I need right now," Gabriel said telling the truth.

Nicholas ordered him a double and then they talked.

"How did it go?" Nicholas asked sternly but not really wanting to hear.

"Very sad, I'm afraid. His mother fainted at the grave. I don't understand why people do that to themselves. She had to stand there and watch the casket being lowered. No wonder she collapsed, I almost did."

"That's a shame, she's such a sweet woman. Did a lot of people show up, you know, like a lot of his friends from the bar?" Nicholas asked.

"Yes, I think all of New Town was there," Gabriel said.

"Hmm, I'm sure his father loved that. He was there too, wasn't he?"

"Yes, I think so. I really don't know his father. Just his mother. She's a client of mine."

"His father recently found out about Sam, when Sam went into the hospital. Needless to say, it didn't go over very big, with daddy. Sam told me this after he got out of the hospital the first time." Nicholas paused, then began again as he stared deeply into Gabriel's deep-sea green eyes, "Sam had been sick for about three years before he went into the hospital. Did you know that?"

"No. Actually I only knew Sam for a little over a year. God, he never looked sick."

"Well, he was, and he kept it secret from most people. It's a slow burn of a disease, baby." Nicholas was beginning to feel pissed as he discussed the matter, but he knew he needed to go on with it. "Sam was taking AZT on and off during the three years, and that shit really started fucking him up. His bone marrow booked, if you know

181

what I mean. He had to have one blood transfusion after another, and then the quacks started quacking about bone marrow transplants and chemotherapy. Can you believe that! An already shot immune system and they wanted to start pumping him up with some other kind of poisons."

"Why did Sam keep it a secret? I know that sounds stupid, but we were becoming fairly close, and all-- he never even suggested the possibility to me. Maybe I could have helped. Somehow," Gabriel said and sipped his drink. He stared, as though thoughtlessly, or just the opposite, into the mirror over the bar.

"Sam told exactly three people: Gary, the owner of the Force, his priest who is also queer, and *moi*. And he made us swear on Judy Garland's eternal soul that we would breathe not a word."

"He did not."

"Most certainly, he did."

"No, I mean about Judy Garland."

"Oh yes. Judy was his patron saint, sweetie. And although that may seem dated to you, Sam was quite a camp in his day. Anyway, if you two were, oh, how did you put it, becoming fairly close, you should have known all about Campy Sam. I'm surprised La Judy wasn't singin' at the wake."

"Well, I didn't know all about that."

"Anyway, Sam was desperately afraid to be stared at, you know, made a spectacle of. He didn't want to be constantly under the watchful eye of everyone constantly wanting to help. You know what I mean, like, oh Sam, do you really think you should have that drink, or that cigarette, or that cup of coffee, or that hand job, or whatever the hell it is he wanted."

Gabriel was silent, contemplative.

Nicholas continued, "He was also desperately in fear of *being* fear itself. A lot of people, gays too, can be pretty insensitive about someone who is HIV positive you know."

"It's just out of ignorance," Gabriel said.

"Yeah, ignorance and bliss. A winning combination. Opened up a lot of graves, let me tell you."

"And shut a lot of mouths, too," Gabriel said and smiled. He then asked, "Why did you leave so abruptly last night at the funeral home? You didn't even say goodbye."

Nicholas turned his face away from the angel. Looking into the great antique mirror over the bar, he stared at the two of them sitting together. He thought: *we look good together.*

"I'm sorry," Nicholas apologized, "that was very rude, but I was very upset." He looked back at Gabriel.

And Gabriel asked again, "What was all that about your filmmaker friend? The whole thing sounded a little weird. I mean like the conversation was out of place."

"It was out of place, Gabriel, like in outer space. Just forget about it. Anyway lunch is on Matthew, the filmmaker friend."

"Well, that's nice, considering I'm kind a low on the dough," Gabriel said and finished his drink.

"Another?" invited Nicholas.

"Why not," Gabriel smiled.

"But, I would like to meet him. Matthew, I mean," insisted Gabriel.

183

"We'll see. It's a possibility," Nicholas said as he attempted to flag the bartender. "I think we're invisible," he said wanting to change the subject.

"I love film. What's he made? You mentioned he's well known."

"Well known, in some circles, I said," Nicholas said.

"Sound's a touch elitist," Gabriel said as Nicholas ordered the drinks.

"It's what?" Nicholas turned again toward Gabriel.

"Elitist. Your friend and his some circles."

"Gabriel, if you have to know, Matthew makes gay porn films. There, that's it. Out in the open."

Silenced, Gabriel turned away to look again into the mirror.

"I love gay porn films." Gabriel smiled at Nicholas by way of the mirror. "That's why you wanted me to meet him." Turning to look at Nicholas directly he continued, "You didn't want me to cut Matthew's hair at all, did you? You were going to arrange a meeting to see if your friend wanted to use me in a film. Is that it, Nicholas?" The pink in Gabriel's face faded to ivory.

"Actually," Nicholas began as the drinks arrived, "the truth is, Matthew is rather old and from time to time, when his needs are such, I procure for him. He pays me well, and it's usually very little trouble. I'm not the casting agent for Matthew's films, you see, but for him, for his pleasure. So I thought I would bring you to him; he's really very kind and very generous. But, then I thought again.

"Since we met, you and I, there has been no greater difficulty than getting you out of my mind. Believe me, I have tried everything, because this feeling you've caused, which I've experienced only once before is, I have tried as successfully as possible to convince myself, too dangerous to deal with. *Love*, you know Gabriel, is not a many splendored thing. It can very well be a prelude to the most dreadful unhappiness.

"Anyway, as far as I can understand, you are exactly what Matthew desires, but you see, Gabriel, you are exactly what I desire as well."

With that, Nicholas reached his hand to Gabriel's face lightly brushing the boy's cheek with his fingers. At once, pink blushed the silken skin, as if Nicholas had painted it there with rose watercolor.

24

∞

Lemon light of the spring sun, suffused through the dusty glass of the skylights above them, softly illuminated the table where Nicholas and Gabriel had been seated.

They ordered steak au poivre, pommes frites, and Caesar salad for two, a specialty of the restaurant prepared at the table. A bottle of Pinot Noir had been happily accepted at the suggestion of the waiter.

"You seem much better this afternoon than you sounded on the phone this morning," Gabriel commented as the waiter departed.

"I was a wreck," Nicholas said. "It's embarrassing, I usually don't behave that way."

"No, what I meant was, I'm happy to see that you appear so happy."

"Appearances do not necessarily the truth make."

"Then, you don't feel well, is that it?"

"Let's just say, I am stabilizing." And Nicholas lifted his glass of wine and drank. "To your health," he said and they both drank together then, touching glass to glass, before lips.

"May I ask you something personal? Of course you can tell me to fuck off if you want," Gabriel began.

Nicholas nodded.

"How long has it been since-- he died?" Gabriel's body tightened imperceptibly.

Nicholas said, "David, you mean?"

Gabriel nodded.

"A year. Two years. A century," Nicholas sighed and looked down into the blood-red wine shimmering in his glass. "It still makes me very sad when I think about it," he said. But, his eyes brightened as he brought them back to Gabriel's eyes. "You have," Nicholas praised him almost awesomely, "the most strangely beautiful eyes I have ever seen."

Gabriel said, "Thank you," and felt mystified by Nicholas's attention.

Very suddenly, as if by some magic spell he thought, his long awaited wish was coming true. If it were to come true with Nicholas, then it could not be better.

"Let's not talk about it then," Gabriel suggested.

"Sometimes, you know, I need to talk about it. I've done a very good job about keeping it all bottled up, for a very long time," Nicholas said and paused, then went on, "I have a friend, Gabriel, and her name is Anais. She was very close to David and still is to me. She's a writer, an intellectual, very deep my friend Anais is. But, for various and unfortunate reasons, she is hellishly unhappy. She lives in hell most of the time, but if you didn't really know her well enough, you would never suspect this from the way she portrays herself. She has, as most writers I suppose do, invented herself, her exterior public self that is. Anyway, for a good long time I've shared the same address as Anais. But unlike her, my public performance hasn't been quite so subtle. She opened my eyes to that fact, a few nights ago, as we spent the evening together in blissful distress. And it suddenly became all too terribly apparent to me, that she and I were neighbors in a ghetto where I did not belong. I have, since that night, come to realize Gabriel, that hell is not the place where I wish to live out the rest of my days."

"Sometime, for some people, Nicholas, grief takes longer to deal with and is handled in different ways you know," Gabriel said.

"So true," Nicholas said. "And you, I know, are no stranger to that."

"Yes, you're right. I also know that everybody has strengths cut from the same fabric, but sewn into different patterns. We are, you know, all part of a great cosmic web that has no weaver," Gabriel said smiling secretively. He sipped some wine.

Nicholas sipped some too, and lit a cigarette and said, "How metaphysical of you. If it wasn't for the absence of the crystal around your neck, I would have thought that I was dining with Shirley MacLaine."

"Surely you might be," Gabriel said coyly. "Anyway, I read a great deal, Nicholas. Books inspire me. They help me to cope with what I consider to be an otherwise inhospitable reality."

"And I thought booze was for that," Nicholas said as he refilled his emptying wine glass.

"That too, except books usually do not give one as bad a hangover," Gabriel said and lifted his glass for replenishment.

"Who is your favorite author?" Nicholas asked as he poured.

"I don't know to say that I have one; I have so many," Gabriel said, "but if I had to, I probably would say,

Tennessee Williams. I think he has always hit the nail right on its dark little head."

"But," Nicholas said, "he was a playwright. Aside from playwrights who is your favorite?"

"You do know that he published short stories?"

"Did he?"

"Yes, he did. But playwrights I think are the greatest authors. Because if they're good, really good I mean, they get right down into the marrow of the bone, you know, and isn't that the whole thing about writing?"

"I suppose. You can't get much deeper than that," Nicholas said. "It makes sense, though," he continued, "that you admire Williams. I mean after all, your life, from what little I know about it, sounds exactly like one of his dramas."

"Yes," Gabriel acknowledged the fact wistfully, in a revelatory way, "it does seem like that really, doesn't it?"

"Don't tell me that has never occurred to you?" Nicholas asked him.

"I don't think as much as it has occurred to you, actually," Gabriel said, appearing a bit lost in thought.

"You know, from the look on your face, I believe that this *strange* coincidence agrees with you," Nicholas toyed with him.

"Who is your favorite author?" Gabriel asked, jibbing the subject back to Nicholas.

"*I am living at the Villa Borghese. There is not a crumb of dirt anywhere, nor a chair misplaced. We are all alone here and we are dead,*" Nicholas said as if reading from the book.

"What a scream," Gabriel broke into laughter, "and I thought I was the only person I knew who's read Henry Miller."

"You know this?" Nicholas appeared more dazzled than Gabriel.

"Of course, *The Tropic of Cancer*," Gabriel said.

"Almost very good," Nicholas praised and pressed his foot against Gabriel's, under the table, "It's *Tropic of Cancer*, you can dispense with the *The*," and he winked at the boy.

"Smart ass. Yes, I've read Henry. He's a bit less desperate than Tennessee I think," Gabriel said.

"That, dear one, is because Henry wasn't a queen," Nicholas offered. "He didn't come sufferin' from out that same queenly pathos we all know and do so love, so very much," Nicholas said in a slow southern drawl.

And after the waiter prepared the salad and served it on iced glass plates Gabriel asked, "Do you want my anchovy, Nicholas? I hate them," he said.

"My dear boy, don't you know that it is a certain sin against nature to eat a Caesar salad without the anchovy?" Nicholas said reaching his fork toward the fishy delicacy. "By all means, I will take your anchovy, but it makes me wonder just how pedestrian you truly are." Nicholas smiled patting Gabriel's hand.

"Let me tell you then," Gabriel said and began again saying: "Cindy Saliva was sitting in the Fabulous Ice Cream Parlor, fourth floor, Marshall Fields, State Street, gorging herself on a Super Fantastic Hot Fudge Banana Split. In walks Laverne Lipshits, her most lovingly hated best friend. Seeing Cindy sitting there Laverne says, Cindy darling, I thought you were on a diet. Why are you gorging yourself on that Super Fantastic Hot Fudge Banana Split? Cindy looks up at Laverne and retorts through a chocolated mouthful: Eat shit, Lipshits."

And Nicholas, hit with laughter, found his fish lost in flight as it fell from his fork to the floor.

"Touché!" Nicholas cheered. "And, oh how very clever of you."

"You liked that, eh?" Gabriel said beaming as he began eating.

"Much too much," Nicholas said.

"Gabriel," Nicholas began, "you're so different than I had imagined you to be, the night we met."

"How do you mean?" he asked.

"Your silence that night at the bar was odd I thought. And the reason why I felt that way is because I didn't take you for being shy or unintelligent. Unconventional, I was sure, but your silence was disconcerting," Nicholas said.

"I was a bit stoned and getting drunk, I guess. When I saw you, you hit me as being something quite unbelievable, someone very unusual. It's hard for me to talk about this, but you remind me, physically that is, of Sebastian my stepfather. You're younger-- but, nonetheless you--" and his voice trailed off and his eyes penetrated the eyes of Nicholas.

They stopped eating for a moment, each caught and held in the other's ocular embrace. And the sun's light, thready and golden, cast down through the windows above them, played upon the glass and silver and white china on the table, spinning itself into a delicate rainbow tapestry in the air around them.

"I feel very beautiful being with you, Nicholas," Gabriel said.

"You are very beautiful Gabriel," Nicholas said.

"No, I don't mean looks. I mean, inside," said Gabriel.

"Take the compliment, dummy, it's true," Nicholas said.

"Thank you," spoke the angel, "so are you."

"Gabriel," Nicholas asked as he sipped his wine, "do you believe in God?"

"From the look on your face I guess this one's not about Oona's dog," and he paused and drank from his glass. "Nicholas, that's a tough one. Sometimes I do, I guess, and other times I don't, but, mostly I think I really do."

"Why do you? I mean, how can you, with all that you say you've gone through, and with all that you see people go through? If there is a God, you know, like they talk about, God the Loving Father, God the All Caring and all of that, why would this God be playing such a nasty game. Right down to the Jesus story, it all seems such a nasty game. Let's face it, even the big league angels are all screwed up, never mind the writers of those there *inspired* Words."

"What do you mean?" Gabriel asked.

"Well," Nicholas began, "once upon a time, in the little Town o' Bethlehem, there was this archangel named Gabriel, you remember him? A couple thousand years ago, once upon a time, our winged hero sees Little Miss Mary Quite Contrary all puffed up with no place to go. Whispering into the bedeviled ear of good old Joey boy, her husband about not to be, he tells him to chill, that his darling little wife has really been *shtupped* by God, after all, and not by some fornicator. Hallelujah, she's pregnant with the Son of God, not the fornicator's! All is forgiven she can stay. Thirty-three years later Sonny Boy has a blind date with the old rugged cross, and thank ya, Jeezus-- Christianity!

"Now, not too long down the road from this quaint little bedtime story, you've got Gabriel again, but this time he's flapping his wings like a berserk windmill in the darkness of an antediluvian cave, and uttering the whisperings of some new madness into the ear of this crazy desert cat's head. Allah be praised-- Islam! Both stories contradict each other, right down to how you should take a piss, so who's right: Gabriel Number One or Gabriel Number Two?"

"Keep going, Nicholas, and you'll end up like Salman Rushdie," said Gabriel number three. "Anyway it sounds like a new television game show. Better than Jeopardy. I think you're on to something truly rewarding."

"Yes, and perhaps we could get Salman out of hiding to host it. We could call it, Blaspheme That Angel."

"Better yet," Gabriel said laughing, "how about, Up Your Ideology."

"I like that," Nicholas said happily, "that I like."

"So," asked Gabriel, "how is it that you and God parted company?"

And as the waiter removed himself from their table after bringing out the perfectly prepared steaks, Nicholas began to speak of his past.

While they ate, while Nicholas spoke, Gabriel remained silent listening to the words, as Nicholas had listened to his, the night it rained.

"Even the earliest memories of my childhood are not happy ones. When I was about five years old, I remember sitting by the table in the kitchen, talking to my mother.

"My mother was a very sad person who was filled with anxiety and resentfulness. But, she siphoned off her hatred and phobias onto other people, with the help of her church, not to mention a considerable amount of her bank account to those big shots in the church.

"Mother was recently widowed, and I know that she missed my father desperately. She tried to keep her unhappiness hidden, beneath an iron facade, believing that father was just around the heavenly corner, but you could see her seething, practically foaming at the mouth.

"Anyway, I remember being in the kitchen; she was probably scolding me. She showed me her finger, my mother, and said, 'Look there, see, I've grown a wart. What do you think I should do about this good for nothing wart, Nicholas?' I told her to cut it off with a knife. And she did it! She took out a knife and cut the damn thing right off. But you don't cut off a wart with a kitchen knife-- remember, I was only five years old when I offered this profound medical advice.

"Three days later, my mother comes to me with her hand covered with gauze and Band Aids. 'It's infected,' she yells. 'You told me to cut it off!' And she grabs me hard by my ear pulling me into my room and BANG she slams the door shut behind me. 'Read the bible!' she screams from the other side of the door. My mother. How do you like that? Funny, I guess she didn't realize that you can't really read the bible when you're five.

"My grandmother, her mother, said that she loved me. She told me how mother really cared and all of that crap. But I can honestly say that I never felt that from her, no warmth, not much of anything really, except criticism.

"I know it sounds strange, but I cannot remember her coming to me and putting her arms around me. No hugs, no kisses. I was shocked to find out that mothers did those things.

"You see, good old mom had been desensitized by religion. She was, for all intents and purposes, a bit of a fanatic. Mother was in love with Jesus and not much else. We didn't own a t.v., that was the devil's plaything of course, so I really didn't know what mothers did, except mine that is, until I was allowed one afternoon, to go to a friend's home after school.

"'Billy, darling,' his mother greeted her son, my friend, at the door beaming, 'how are you, did you have a nice day at school?' And she put her arms around him and gave him a great big hug and kiss. I was stupefied. It made me feel giddy, this scene did, like when you're just beginning to get drunk.

"When I got older and left home I had very little contact with my mother. I saw her briefly when I returned from Europe and just after I met David. But after that, deliberately, there was no attempt on either my or her part to make contact. We just had nothing in common.

"Then she became very sick; she was dying I was told, so I went to see her once more, and for the very last time. This was an awful occasion for me. I saw my mother every day until she died, but even as this woman lie dying on her bed, she was the same overbearing, unyielding dictator that she had always been. She would yell nonsense and spew accusatory remarks about how I would burn in hell for rejecting her and her God. Over and over my mother would insist that soon she would be in heaven. Reunited with my father, who had died many years before, she proclaimed with her last breath that they would be remarried by Jesus himself and live together for eternity, while I would roast in hell.

"And then she died, my dear mother, in a very strange silence that seemed for her so unfitting, her face swept with rapture.

"You know, from time to time, when I am in bed alone and can't fall asleep, I think about her. I think about how I have, for the most part, reconciled myself with the world, that there is no one I truly hate, that I have no one to hate. And then I wonder how it can be, that I cannot think well at all of this woman who just happened to be my mother.

"So I say to myself: what if *you* die tonight, while you're sleeping, Nicholas. Suppose there is an afterlife and you bump into her. What are you going to say when you come face to face? *Nothing*. That's it. Because she will always have the final disparaging word."

They sat together then in a shared moment of silence. Nicholas thinking of how things might have been with a mother of his own choosing; Gabriel wondering how it felt to have a real mother, at all.

"It's a sad story, Nicholas," Gabriel said almost whispering.

"Yes it is, isn't it? But, not quite as sad as yours. Oona and I had a talk, you know. She helped to fill in the blanks," Nicholas said as he rediscovered the thick filet cooling on his plate. "I talked too much," he said, devouring a piece, "it's turned to ice."

"Mine's delicious," Gabriel said.

"Yes, I can see. What's left of it that is," Nicholas smiled and poured more wine into each glass.

"So, what about God, Nicholas?" Gabriel asked, directing the conversation away from himself. "Is it because of your mother, David, or what? Don't you think that God grant's us free will, so that we can either make it, or break it?"

"Yes, I suppose it's because of mom. Though that's a cheap copout when you think about it. It's really more about my father, who became lost to me before I had a chance to get to know him, who was swept away with cancer like there was no tomorrow. And of course-- yes David, such a believer in God, that he almost made a believer out of me.

"But," and Nicholas shot Gabriel a look that made the angel an instant intimate with the depth of his anger, "it's also about the Paragons of Free Will like, Mr. Adolf Meat Tenderizer Hitler, God's gift to the free thinkers and the Jews; The Fascinating Fascist Mr. Mussolini, Free Will Wheeler and Dealer, who could command eviscerations with simultaneous castrations; and let's not forget the ever popular Big Joe Stalin, who got rid of more people than old Benito and Adolf put together.

"Yes, Gabriel, if God grants free will, it just always seems that it's a gift given to the wrong people.

197

And don't forget, sweetie, this is the gift of free will, signed, sealed, and delivered by the God of *love*."

"But I don't think it's really like that. I mean, I believe that there are unforeseen plans at work in the world, which people are just not meant to understand," Gabriel said.

"I can't buy that; it's too naive. It's exactly what all religions are based on. The poor fucks who succumb to the free will of monsters, for the most part, in their terror, always try to comfort themselves with that stuff of religion," Nicholas said as he finished the steak.

"Nicholas, even if this God we're talking about is an absolute hoax, sometimes it's just what people need to give them hope, to help them carry on," said Gabriel. "And what's so wrong about that?"

"Because, I believe it's a dreadful deception, which I do not think hope should be. The poppies, Gabriel, of the wicked witch of the west, which put Dorothy to sleep in the pretty garden of fear, is not hope." Nicholas winked and lit a Salem.

"What about the snow of Glenda?" asked Gabriel.

"The snow of Glenda, maybe, but definitely not the poppies," Nicholas answered.

"You better watch out before someone drops a house on you," Gabriel Billie Burked.

"And your little dog too," cackled Nicholas.

"So, what'll we do now, Nietzsche?" Gabriel asked as he wiped his hands with his napkin, disposing it to the china plate.

"I think it's time for dessert," Nicholas laughed, "and some *cafe*, and then how about a walk by the lake?"

And Gabriel said, "You're on."

25

∞

"Have you ever been to Santa Cruz?" Nicholas asked Gabriel.

They walked slowly, side by side, both taking in the grand oceanic expanse of Lake Michigan. The warm summery afternoon air, drifting in long lazy currents, circled around them like geriatric ghosts.

"No," said Gabriel, "I've never been to California. Got this thing about earthquakes."

Several distant sailboats, what could have been tiny origami masterpieces, bobbed with grace upon the unusually calm blue-green lake.

"I can't believe they're out there with boats already," remarked Nicholas.

"Yeah," Gabriel said, "it feels like summer, but who would trust it?"

"Natalie Wood," answered Nicholas.

Gabriel looked at him and laughed and said, "Oh, Jesus, what a lousy joke."

"I kinda liked it," Nicholas said. "Want to hear one more?"

"If I must," Gabriel smiled.

"Alright. What kind of wood doesn't float?" he asked.

"Oh, God," Gabriel breathed.

"Natalie Wood," Nicholas said.

"Please," Gabriel begged painfully, "enough, I can't take any more."

"I don't think I *would* either," Nicholas agreed. "So," he asked, "you've got quake paranoia, is that it?"

"Well, to tell you the truth, Nicholas, if I go that far west, I'm stopping in Nevada. I love the desert and I'd love to see Las Vegas," Gabriel said beaming like a child in a candy store whose gotten away with some small sweet theft.

"You're joking!" Nicholas said and he stopped to light a cigarette, "I was seriously thinking about moving there."

"Really?" enthused Gabriel, "what a riot, so was I!"

"Thought it might be fun to work in a casino, be a Black Jack dealer. The goddamn place never shuts off and the booze is free," Nicholas said taking a drag off the Salem. "Sure you don't want one?" he offered a cigarette to Gabriel.

"No thanks. I'm doing better than I imagined about this quitting thing," Gabriel said.

"It's really working?"

"Yeah, it's real work, but I'm starting not to miss them. I'm not kidding," he said, attempting to convince the doubtful stare.

"Hmm," Nicholas said, "maybe that's not such a bad idea. I might give it a try," and he paused, then put his arm around Gabriel's shoulders. "You'll help?" he asked.

"You don't have to ask, Nick."

Nicholas hugged Gabriel to him for a moment, then removing his arm, he let the boy go.

And by that tiny change in the way Gabriel had said his name, the two of them became closer.

"Why did you ask me about Santa Cruz?" Gabriel asked.

"Because I was watching the seagulls circling in the sky over the lake, and the air smells fresh and fishy like the ocean. And suddenly this reminded me of the time we were there, in Santa Cruz, walking along the cool white beach on that hot blue summer afternoon."

"You and David?" Gabriel asked carefully, but kept looking forward as they walked with slow quiet steps.

"Yes," he said distantly, "with David." He then continued, "Santa Cruz is on the ocean, there's a boardwalk there, and running along the ocean, near the boardwalk, is a very colorful picturesque amusement park, like a rainbow stretched out on the ground, like something out of a movie. It would be perfect for a movie," he said with solemn authority.

Nicholas stopped walking and said, "Let's sit. It's very pleasant here."

And they both sat close together occupying a large flat rock on the esplanade, their bodies touching.

"You know, Gabriel, I've never really liked Chicago, even though I've been here for quite some time, but I have always loved to sit on the shore and look at Lake Michigan. It's like looking at the ocean."

"It is beautiful. I can't believe all that ice melted so quickly. This weather's sort of weird, don't you think?"

"Well, what do you expect. It's Chicago," Nicholas said laughing.

"Chicago's not that bad, Nick. It's better than Detroit," Gabriel said.

"No comment," said Nicholas.

Sea gulls and pigeons and an assortment of other less notable birds mingled on the beach. The dirty sand there, ladened with mankind's thoughtless disrespect for its ecological well being, provided those birds with a delightfully never ending but all too tragic unremoveable feast.

An overweight couple on a bicycle-built-for-two flew by. The woman in the rear, wearing a GO CUBS tee shirt over her undulating fat, threw her Diet Pepsi bottle in the sand.

"What a fucking pig," Nicholas belched. "God, how I hate that!"

"I hope she falls off that bike on her fat ass," Gabriel joined him.

"That's the ticket," Nicholas jeered, "and I pray her fucking Cubs lose this year!"

"I couldn't agree with you more," Gabriel said and began laughing.

They looked at each other briefly, holding the other in the depths of their eyes. Parting glances, they silently gazed out across the lake, which seemed like an endless sea where the visible plane of the sky and the water became one at the juncture of the horizon.

"So," began Gabriel, "aside from the occupation of procuring young men for your old filmmaker friend, what might be your other profession?" he said, smiling a smart-ass little grin.

"Thought you'd never ask, my child," Nicholas grinned back. "I'm a defrocked attorney," he said. "Whada ya think about that?"

"You talk more like a defrocked priest," Gabriel said. "An attorney, huh. What happened?" he asked.

"It's a long, very long story, but to make shorthand out of it, I got busted for possession of certain illegal drugs. It happened after David's death; I was a mess. Anyway, so, what do I do now? I do a lot of freelance writing for magazines. I've completed a novel, and I am very happy to report, my agent informed me a few days ago that it has been accepted by a New York publishing company. I also happen to have a fairly healthy bank account."

"That's wonderful-- about your book, I mean," Gabriel said. "But you didn't go to jail because of the drug thing?" he asked.

"Nope. I beat the rap, but lost my license to practice law; the judge was a queen, a friend of David and mine.

"I see," Gabriel said coolly.

"Well, don't look so bemused," Nicholas said, "things like that happen all the time. Anyway, you're no Little Miss Innocent, cookie."

"No-- no, I was just thinking it must be awfully sad not to be able to do what you really want to do," Gabriel responded.

"Who says I'm not," Nicholas said. "As a matter of fact, I'm doing exactly what I want to do; practicing law is a big fat pain in the ass, if you want to know the truth of it."

"Really? I thought it would be exciting."

"You can think again. I practiced corporate law and truthfully, if I had to look at one more franchise offering circular, I think I'd shoot myself right between my eyes," Nicholas said as he pointed his fingers, gun like, at Gabriel's forehead.

"I think you were talking about shooting yourself," Gabriel laughed.

"Mmmm, wrong head, you're right," said Nicholas, as he relaxed his hand letting his palm glide gently down along Gabriel's smooth cheek.

Blushing, Gabriel asked, "So, Roy Cohn, what's your novel about?"

"Very funny," Nicholas smiled and said, "It's about an earthling who falls in love with an angel."

"I see," said Gabriel. "A boy or girl angel?" he asked.

"A boy, of course," Nicholas said.

"And what about the earthling, boy or girl?" Gabriel questioned.

"A man," answered Nicholas.

And Nicholas then, very lovingly, put his arms around Gabriel, holding the boy in an adoring embrace. Kissing him gently on the mouth they felt each other's warm yearning.

It was true about the earthling and the angel. In the Gods' smiling eyes their reflection gaily sparkled. And as Nicholas let Gabriel go, he kept his stare quite still upon those strange, alluring, Paris green eyes-- eyes that had become gladdened with tears. But, what he saw within them then, as he gazed into the angel's liquid emerald eyes, was not poison, but heaven.

"You see," Gabriel said blinking, "I could start crying, you touched my heart," he quickly wiped his eyes with his hand. Nicholas took Gabriel's hand and kissed his fingers where the tears had made them moist.

Gabriel smiling, laughed meekly, not knowing where to look; a gesture which declared the uncertainty of response, a registration of excitement and unanticipated yet delicious embarrassment.

"So," he began, as Nicholas released his warm hand, "what's your novel really about?"

"Didn't buy that, huh? Oh, well," Nicholas said displaying a controlled disarming smile of self-confidence. "The truth is, it's about friendships," he went on, "and how they live and how they perish, and how some of them actually survive. It's also very autobiographical."

"Tell me more," Gabriel said as he studied the angled planes of Nicholas's face, as Nicholas looked out to the lake observing its splendid magnificence.

He lit a cigarette and began to disclose parts of his life which had solidified into one long written account.

"I've titled it," began Nicholas, "*Memoir of an Amnesiac*. It has to do with friendships and relationships. Some of these narratives are about the people like us-- you know, the best part of the population, which is said to be at least ten-percent. Other of these stories, entirely different scenarios.

"But the point of the novel, its reason so to speak, is its dealings with the loss of friendship and the mechanisms behind the act of this loss. I have, Gabriel, lost many friends through my own fault, a loss which I consider a great misfortune and mistake. These friends, who are still very much alive, I truly miss. I suppose this novel is my profound apology to them." And Nicholas shut his eyes becoming quiet and still, as if in prayer.

"One of the stories in the book is about a long lost friend of mine named Kurt." And he opened his eyes.

"Years ago, I had a roommate and we lived, well I think I told you, not too far from where you live now," Nicholas said, looking at Gabriel, and Gabriel nodded.

"My friend, this roommate, his name was Kurt. Kurt was a very smart guy you understand, good looking, well built but getting fat from lack of exercise and eating too much; he was German, but told everyone including Jesus Christ, that he was a Jew. He spoke self-taught German with a native-like fluency, and he tried to teach me, but instead I learned some Yiddish from him, which he also knew.

"Kurt was the only person I have ever known to actually sleep with his telephone as if it were a teddy bear. He and his phone were practically inseparable; all the loves of his life were constantly calling, or he them, you see, so Kurt established this strange relationship with that phone, treating it like some kind of pet.

"And we were quite good friends at the time, this Kurt and I, and we shared an apartment together, before I met David.

"Anyway, this apartment that we rented, up near Wrigley Field, was a great big dump. It was a cavernous mouse-infested dump with two bedrooms, one of which, Kurt's that is, was converted from the small living room in the front of the place.

"He got most of the furniture, for that second hand bedroom, at second hand shops and Salvation Army resale stores in Uptown and Newtown, and from handouts by people who cared about him, like his boss who happened to be a lesbian and a real Jew. From time to time the two of them had sex, Kurt and his Latvian lesbian boss, in that converted bedroom-- she leaned toward bisexuality, he didn't, so I have no idea what would get him going. And I'll always remember what she said to me when I asked her why they did it. She said: 'A hole's, a hole, Nicholas.' How do you like that?

"Anyway, her name was Iris, but we called her Phoebe, and I used to sing this little song to her, which I think after a while we all thought was a song really about her, and that's why, after all, we started calling her Phoebe. And the song went: *Phoebe Farts has vaginitis. She's a Daughter of Bilitis. She hauls lumber down the pike, that scabby, crabby diesel dyke.*

"Iris thought the song was funny, until one day when I was drunk and performed it for, what I considered to be, the benefit of her mother's amusement, but, alas, with unfortunately just a bit too much candor. Well, *I* thought it was amusing. You see, mom knew all about Iris's friends; she was very *modern* and just *loved* them, but, she was like Helen Keller when it came to the Daughter of Bilitis, and Iris wanted it to stay that way. After that I shelved the song.

"Kurt and Phoebe would come by our place, after work sometimes, and the two of them would get high on some prescription cough syrup, 'loaded with codeine!' Kurt would shriek, that she got from the doctor for her allergies. And they liked to smoke hash, which I once did with them in this shitty little hotel room in Galena, Illinois, while we took a trip there together to witness historical sites. But, instead, we ended up fucked-up on wine and hash and Phoebe's cough syrup, and spent most of the trip in that dark room, taking obscene pictures of each other with Kurt's Polaroid camera, wearing little if any clothing.

"I have to admit, Phoebe was a scream, and our friendship became very tight, which is another story altogether in the novel."

And a cloud obscured Nicholas's face as he said: "Phoebe met this illiterate little lesbian at some feminist function one rainy spring weekend, and the two of them disappeared together forever to Big Dyke Country, Wyoming something like that. Haven't heard one single word from her since. I really miss her, when I think about her, and she doesn't even know who is living or who is dead in our once very close circle of friends. I hope she's still one of the living," he ended, and the cloud disappeared.

"Anyway, back to Kurt, if you are still interested," Nicholas said to Gabriel.

Gabriel nodded his head, smiling.

"So, Kurt and I had this friend, who came to live with us in the dump, one summer. Actually, this friend, a vanished friend of mine from days gone by, who I hadn't seen in at least a year or two, suddenly reemerged into my life one night with startling clarity. And it just so happened that Kurt and I were together that night, in this gay bar called Alphies, on Rush Street, when Paul The Invisible made his unimpassioned exit from the ladies room. And she *was* a Lady, let me tell you; a lady in waiting: for the operation, you see."

"What was she waiting for?" Gabriel asked.

"For welfare to pay for it. She rarely if ever had a dime, but she did have balls, that drag queen did. I called her a drag queen to her face, of course, because she never made the change, completely that is, and as far as I know to this day, never did. So I thought the title befitting.

208

"She did have *tiny* tits though, like a pubescent girl on the verge of something big, the result, I imagine, of hormone injections and pills and the like-- whatever it is that they take. And I did see those Little Tits of Shame, once, that summer on the roof of the dump, while she and I were up there sunbathing and drinking Screwdrivers. I convinced her to take off her top, that *no*, of course I wouldn't laugh, how could you think I would laugh, dear? Anyway she did, and I did! I couldn't help it. Well, with the booze and those tits like that, who wouldn't?

"Anyway Paula, nee Paul; aka Tasha, short for Natasha-- there you have it, the bestowing of The Names, that night became Kurt's friend as well. Lucky Kurt.

"Overdone bursts of tremendous cheer went up between us like fireworks as our eyes met. Though, in reality, I actually wanted to run out the door with Kurt in tow, because, you see, Tasha liked to swill it down, but as I said before, never had the bucks. She was a fast drinking, sweet talking, drink hustler, you know what I mean. And I must admit, she did well with the older queens, which is why she hung around the wrinkle rooms, like The Haig, which like Alphies, no longer exists.

"So there we were, reunited, Tasha and I, but now we are a *menage a trois*, a la Kurt. And Tasha, who after I buy her a drink, of course, begins to gladden our hearts with the sad and most touching tale of her two-year hiatus from the world at large. Woe is she.

"Let me tell you, two years have gone by between us, and the drag queen is still singing the same old shtik: no job, no love, no money, nowhere to go-- oy vey! kinda makes you want to run out and buy a gun. But, Kurt is hooked; his eyes are glazing over fast. Now he buys her a

209

drink, and another, and another. Soon he'll be kissing her hand, opening the door for her, holding her chair when she sits, inviting her out for din din, giving her a charity fuck-- bringing her home to live! Which he does. With my approval, of course.

"Kurt assures me that we've got ourselves a houseboy-- he'll help us cook and clean, Kurt tells me, but what we've really got, and I ought to know, is a full-of-talk-and-big-ideas, lazy, live-in drag queen, who will eat and drink us out of house and dump.

"So the three of us plan Tasha's future with us at the dump, no one planning harder or happier than she. We say that she can stay with us for free, if she does the houseboy thing and goes to school like she says she wants to. And we sit there in that dark joint, knocking back the Jack Daniels, getting drunker, listening to Donna Summer singing *Love To Love You Baby*, and smoking one cigarette after another.

"Tasha, by the way, was a Marine for four years, talk about a few good men. She has veteran's benefits corning out the ass, she tells us. And what she plans to do with them, when she gets them, she makes it very clear, is to go to Columbia College down on South Michigan Avenue and study painting and writing. Oh happy day! The very essence of the word *direction* is gleaming in her droopy alcoholized brown eyes. She has found her niche; she is on her way.

"Ah, but I know better. I have heard this all before, and what else I know is that she *is* on her way, that much is true; however, the direction that she is about to pursue is directly related to the second, or third, or maybe even fifth-hand sofa, which has been falling apart bit by bit, for the last year, in our lovely north-side dinning room.

"Yes, Tasha moves in. And no, she most certainly does not become our houseboy. What this Miss Natasha Thing, aspiring painter and writer becomes, is our Day Sleeper.

"Funny how alcohol stimulates the enthusiasm gland. Oh, she just couldn't wait, that night at Alphies, to tackle those pots and pans with soap and water, become Le Chef at Chez Dump, wring out the dirty laundry and hang it up to dry. Even the Marines that night, a whole platoon even, couldn't have kept her away from Columbia to get her artistic career rolling.

"But, Tasha was a gas, this I must admit. Through all of the crap it always seemed fun. And fun is, what fun is, not really anything more than that; so eventually the Day Sleeper became like fun, nothing serious about her at all, which after all, is very serious.

"One day, one amazing auspicious day, Tasha The Great finally made it to Columbia College and applied for her benefits. And like magic, she got them; no questions asked, at least not by many. A certified check in the mail, to be used for living expenses and for school, arrived one day before noon, and thank the lord the postman rang twice, or our Tasha would have been SOL as they say. Sleeping Beauty awakened and received her reward, and she told me later, rewarded the mail man with a blow job, how's that for a tip!

"Now, what does our hero, Miss Natasha Day Sleeper Thing do with these big bucks? She goes on a shopping spree down Halsted Street, hitting all the vintage clothing stores, and empowers herself with a queenly arsenal of vintage drag queen artillery, like-- a short black taffeta and silk dress wet with black sequins, which she

211

gaily proclaims is her black magic party dress; several handbags, one she swears was swung by Tallulah Bankhead; makeup; fashion eye glasses; a Jackie O pill box hat, with veil; several pairs of CFMPs, including one pair of cha cha heels that Miss Thing says she'll wear when we go dancing at Carols, *gee thanx*, et cetera, et cetera.

"Of course neither Kurt nor I count, we don't merit a fucking thing; we just keep the drag queen well fed and well liquored-up, that's all-- who'd expect even a token gesture of simple, quiet, noble, understated drag queen sentiment?

"So, this endless list finally ends with school in mind. Tasha, with the last of her change, remembers Columbia! and gets her pale yellow artistic hands on an old brown leather portfolio, into which, she says with determination, she will house all her art work. Fascinating! But, she doesn't have any-- art work, that is. Though assuring us that she will once she starts school, I implore: 'Tasha, my sweet, how can you start school when you have spent every thin dime of the good taxpayers money on your Drag Queen Circus?'

"'Oops! I forgot all about that,' her drooping puppy dog eyes roll around in her head. She gushes in a poorly done Marilyn Monroe whisper, 'Oh well, just have to wait for the next check-- love that mail man!' And she walks away from me, swishing her ass, singing, 'A kiss on the hand may be quite continental, but a *blow job* is a girl's best friend.'

"It's just about this time, in Tasha's dreamy little dream world, that Kurt begins to tug on the wire which has allowed La Swordette of Damocles to dangle ever so precariously over Miss Thing's carefully coifed head. In other words, Kurt has had it with her shit, a situation I had

212

been waiting for for quite sometime, and he decides that it's about time for things to change. So he sits down with our dearly beloved, longing to be loved drag queen, and has with her, what he refers to as, a father daughter chat. To set things aright, you see.

"At this point, I really couldn't care less what happens. Kurt got us into this mess, now if he wishes, he can get us out. Simple as that I think.

"So, while father knows best, I am in my bedroom, immodestly sipping brandy and watching some old Bette Davis movie on the old tellie, you know, the one where she says: *'What a dump,'* which, considering the surroundings that surrounded me then, could not have been uttered at a more appropriate time.

"From the dinning room-- The Place of Greatest Darkness; the Heart of the Haunted House; that forbidden zone were within the drag queen sleeps by day, I hear her choking sobs ebb and flow in a convulsive vocalization that sounds more like yodeling than crying. It reminds me of the time I saw her do an unplanned, unrehearsed drag number at a bar called The Artful Dodger, somewhere on Milwaukee Street, in that hell hole of a neighborhood known as Wicker Park. She sang, or rather, she yodeled the Grace Jones song, *I Need A Man*, but what she got was a barrage of pennies thrown at her from the audience like a copper asteroid shower. One of those lucky pennies, flung with all the skill of a ballistics expert, found the source of the trouble, ending up in Tasha's big mouth, putting a cork on her show-stopping tune.

"And as I sat in my dark room, brandy sipping in front of my little black and white television, watching Bette Davis wave around her cigarette, and listening to the Singing None out yonder, I was hoping with all the

213

expectation a child musters for the arrival of Santa Claus on Christmas morn, that this very same penny saving act of the Gods would happen again posthaste, choking our Tasha to death. But, her oeuvre I soon discovered, was limitless.

"I sucked up every drop of brandy in the bottle, that night, delivering myself from the unbearable light-headedness of being in the same house with that voice. In the morning, over coffee and *schmerz*, daddy Kurt informs me that our loved one has dearly departed. He kicked her ass out, late last night, he tells me, after she kept bullshitting him he said."

"And what did she do then?" asked Gabriel.

"Kurt, the ever thoughtful, would not allow Tasha to disturb me, but he granted her permission to use the phone, which she did of course, with alacrity. Like a conjurer, she summoned up one of her drag queen apostates, apostasy, in that this one, I understand, was a true change, an authentic sexual defector, reassigned to a new loyalty so to speak, in accordance with all the known laws of the unknown transsexual universe.

"On a broom she flew to collect our Miss Natasha and together they took off into the night like the witches that they were, and I have not heard one word about her, or from her, since."

"That's hysterical, what a scream." Gabriel was laughing. "And what happened after that?" he asked.

"Ah, shortly after the departure of Miss Thing's Flying Drag Queen Circus, Kurt and I departed for Europe.

"We took a trip, together, to Germany and France; we stayed in gay hostels when we could, and with guys we met in the gay bars there, and we fucked and sucked our way from Heidelberg to Paris, so most of the time we never had to pay for anything. I loved the Paris sites and wanted desperately to stay longer in France, but Kurt broke out with shingles and we had to cut the trip short."

"Shingles, how horrible," Gabriel said. "That doesn't sound too good, if you know what I mean?"

"No it doesn't, but his shingles had nothing to do with AIDS. As a matter of fact, this happened in the seventies, before the term AIDS was even invented.

"So, our picaresque sojourn ended sooner than expected. This was for me fortuitous, because that weekend of my return, I met David.

"Kurt and I arrived at the airport early Saturday evening. He was itching from the herpes and just wanted to rest in his dark bedroom with Teddy the Telephone. I, on the other hand, was itching to go out, which I did, the moment after I threw open the luggage on my bed.

"David was in Chicago visiting friends, and I met him at the baths that night; the rest, of course, is history.

"David lived in San Francisco and he was, at the time, a rather celebrated competition ballroom dancing champion. He, and his partner Karen, owned a dance school there. They were very well known as teachers, and they did tremendously with the school as a business."

"Cha, cha, cha," Gabriel said.

"Yes, indeed. Anyway, there he was, this tall mahogany statue, leaning seductively against the wall of the locker room at the baths, staring at me. The first thing I noticed about him, aside from his blazing white jockstrap-- and I thought about this later-- was not that he was a black man, but that he had the perfectly muscled body of a dancer, which of course he was. His large opalescent eyes, penetratingly blue, seemed electrified with some occult power that not only permitted these eyes to hold such

215

strange color but allowed them to cast such a strange spell as well. Your eyes, Gabriel," Nicholas looked deeply into his eyes, "they have the exact same power." And he looked, again, away.

"It was very magnetic, the feeling that came over me as I moved closer to him. I honestly felt the whole thing out of my control. He had a bright, eager look painted across a boyish face that was almost frighteningly sexual. Never having had sex with a black man before, the thoughts that raced through my mind as I approached him seemed oddly gilt with the essence of the genuinely exotic, nearing that something somehow taboo. This first encounter was really, after all, just like what the tango is, a dance done in celebration of the forbidden. You see, for him, it was no different. I was his first white lover.

"Well it takes two to tango, and David and I did, all night long-- in fact, that entire weekend. And being that it was love at first fuck, I moved to California shortly after our meeting, at his request, to live with him.

"We lived there together, in San Francisco, for seven wonderful years, and, well, you know the rest."

Gabriel, watching Nicholas, nodded, and said nothing.

Nicholas, gazing out across the lake, taking his last drag off his last cigarette, with his eyes carefully fixed upon the flight pattern of the seagulls swimming there in the blushing afternoon sky above the water, said, "David was a very strong, vital, and beautiful man. He was like a seagull with a passion for altitudes high above sea level. He really wasn't frightened of much, not even when he was told he had AIDS, not even when he was dying. As awfully as he did, he just never seemed frightened.

"And I'll always remember what he said to me a few moments before he died. He held onto my hand, as tightly as he could, and looking up at me from his shrunken face his eyes sparkled-- they really did you know, and David said to me, 'Be careful Nicky, I love you very much so please, please take care of yourself.' Then he told me he was so terribly sorry about putting me through all of this, and he closed his eyes; I felt the life go out of his hand, and he died."

A long necessary silence settled momentarily between them then; Gabriel attempting to understand what Nicholas's life was like with David, and now what it had become without this person that he so loved; Nicholas contemplating what life might be like with Gabriel, someone he wanted to, and was falling in love, with.

"I'm sorry, Nicholas," Gabriel said finally. They looked at each other; Gabriel warmly offered him a gentle smile. Taking Nicholas's hand into his, he held it tightly, and Nicholas smiled at the angel, his eyes gladdened with tears.

26

∞

The rain began as unexpectedly as the weather had been strange.

Clouds gathered in the sky above the lake like quick short strokes of gray tempera painted there by a brush. The imperturbable blue of the dome of the lake gave way to a growing tense darkness that dimmed the sun's light. And the wind, just moments before, breezy calm, suddenly bespoke of Thor's fierce pleasure.

All around, people scattered for shelter. But some remained unmoved and quite enchanted by Mother Nature's tough vocabulary. Enjoying her hard Chicago street talk, they appeared undaunted in their own devices.

"Well, you're all wet," Nicholas laughed saying to Gabriel.

"Yeah, and a well's a deep subject, isn't it?" Gabriel laughed back.

"Oh, Christ, we are hitting new lows. I think it's time to get out of the rain," Nicholas said as he stood.

Gabriel stood too, shaking his head; his thick blond hair became a mane of gold wavy curls.

"God," Nicholas breathed as he took Gabriel's face into his hands.

Rain water bathing them washed the angel's face, his long dark eyelashes glistened with a heavy dewy wetness. There was, upon his nose and cheeks, Nicholas discovered just then, a delicate patina of brown freckles which lent the angel face a glow of sensual mischief.

"You are exquisite," he spoke, almost whisperingly to the angelic being. "I know that it probably sounds corny," he sighed, "but, have you ever seen yourself in the rain? You look like a Botticelli."

Gabriel smiled. It was the captivating smile of a beautiful boy, who like the subject of a masterpiece, could only smile that way.

"Let's go to my place, we're not very far," Nicholas invited as he removed his hands from the enticing Botticelli cherub.

And they walked in the rain which poured down from the heavens, lightning sizzling in the sky above them.

Untouched by it all, the earthling and the angel moved to their destination, while the Gods joyfully sang in their hearts of love.

27

∞

S trange eyes.

But they are no longer that, Nicholas mused, as he watched Gabriel move to him.

He recalled just then quite vividly, how he had one night, once thought about those eyes: Paris green, fatal, poison. But, not now. Not at all, he thought. Then, Nicholas smiled.

The rain, he could hear, continued to fall though not as harshly. The lightning and thunder, like the wind, had become indifferent to its rebellious cause, then bored, stumbling wearily to dissipation. A flash and rumble now and again seemed a feeble attempt to startle, simply a cowardly exclamation point arising at the end of an impotent sentence.

The temperature, having dropped considerably outside, introduced a romantic chill to the air where they were within. And, so, the fire that Nicholas had brought to life in the fireplace, crackled and snapped with Christmas jest.

Naked too, Gabriel stood by the bed where Nicholas was, whose arms were wrapped behind his head and propped up by two obese pillows. Uncoiling his arms,

Nicholas reached his hands to Gabriel; taking him, the gripping feel of his heating hands made them both hard.

The boy moved onto the bed, embracing Nicholas, and this time love and desire entwined within them as a thousand realms of existence in a single moment of life.

The God Thor came and painted the bedroom blue in a lustrous momentary intrusion. The amorphous God, so inspired by the beauty of the carnal ballet of the earthling and the angel, revealed himself nearly corporeal in his electric dynamism. Vertiginous ecstasy, the Breath of the Gods, moved upon them then; and at last, as two they became one, both nourished by each other, and at Thor's behest, married by the Gods in an act of glorious delight.

⚜

The rain had stopped, nearly. A light misty drizzle, a half-turn from fog, filled the air like loosely woven gossamer. Red, the color of a ripened peach, spread throughout the early evening April sky. The Gods, blissfully happy with themselves in their act, blushed, just a little.

Nicholas and Gabriel had showered. Now they sat on the sofa together, in the living room, paying their respects to the slowly dying fire. Embers, hissing occasionally, popped like a kettle of popcorn almost ready on the stove. The incense of the fireplace, a smoky woody pine, would linger in that room all night, reminding them of the rain and the wind and their love.

"Look," said Gabriel. And he stood and moved to the long, slim, drapeless windows of the living room. He said, "Come here and look at the sky, Nicholas. It's an unbelievable red, and there's a rainbow. Incredible."

Looking back to Nicholas, who was sipping a glass of champagne, Gabriel extended his arm to him. His hand, floating still in the air, opened in an elegant gesture, so very much like the rendering of the hand of God upon the ceiling of the Sistine Chapel.

Nicholas rose, walked to the beckoning hand, and took it.

"You're right, Gabriel," he said to the angel, holding him close to him, "it is magnificent."

Their eyes, then together, scanned the enchanting sky which enchanted them so very much; the rainbow, arcing above the buildings and trees, played along with the prismatic sunlight, which dancing in the cut glass of the windows, imitated it.

"Beautiful," Nicholas said smiling and kissed Gabriel lightly on his cheek. His smile was as colorful and radiant as the rainbow that had been painted above the city.

"Let's have more champagne," he offered, and moved back to the sofa taking the boy with him by his hand.

"You'll spend the night?" Nicholas asked as he refilled Gabriel's glass.

"I think," Gabriel said as he took the glass of cold gold bubbles, sitting, "you would have a lot of trouble keeping me away."

"Good, that's what I was hoping," Nicholas said.

"You know, Nick, I really don't like champagne very much, but I have to admit that this is delicious."

"Aw, shucks," Nicholas bent his head, imitating shyness, kicking the floor, "it's not this here champagne that tastes so darn good, nope, it's bein' with me that makes the golldarn stuff tickle your tongue so," he laughed. "And ya best say yup to that, boy, or I'll whip your little behind."

"Uh," Gabriel said, "I think you already did, sir."

And they both laughed, drinking the icy, stinging liquid.

"It's time for Jeopardy," Nicholas said as he refilled Gabriel's glass.

He set the sweating bottle back down into the glass bucket of ice, and picking up the little remote control device, the t.v. awakened.

"You watch it too," Gabriel said. "It's the only game show worth watching."

"I know, I love it. I'd like to be on it, but I hate competition, and I'd have to be drunk to do it. You can't play Jeopardy when you're drunk, I have discovered sitting here, watching it drunk and trying to play, so why bother, right?"

"Right. Unless you're Christopher Hitchens," Gabriel answered.

"What?" said Nicholas.

"Christopher Hitchens," Gabriel repeated.

"Good God-- *name dropper*," Nicholas said, and they both laughed, then tuned their attention to the tuned in t.v. program.

The category of the moment was Famous Queens. "Famous Queens for a thousand," said the contestant, a proctologist from Condom, Ohio. The answer: "She is known for her campy, extravagant costumes and jewelry;

223

she lives in Las Vegas and has entertained the world with her talent as a pianist."

"Who is Liberace?" the rectologist instantly replied.

He went on to win the game.

With Jeopardy almost over, Gabriel flipped through the *TV Guide*.

"Oh, this could be fun. Haven't seen it in years," Gabriel said happily.

"What, *Myra Breckenridge* is on tonight?" Nicholas teased.

"No, better than that, *2001*."

"A Space Odyssey," they both said in unison.

"Ah, Kubrick, we'll need pizza or something for this," Nicholas suggested, hungrily licking Gabriel's neck and then up his face.

"Or something," Gabriel said wiping his face with the back of his hand, displaying a pretend look of indignation.

"What, you got something against pizza?" Nicholas said wide eyed.

"No, love," Gabriel hissed coolly, "just a wet face." And he quickly put his glass on the table, and grabbing Nicholas firmly by the shoulders, he pulled him to him kissing him hotly, plunging his tongue into his mouth.

The kiss lasted forever, or something nearly as unimaginable as that.

"Nurse! Doctor! Oxygen, I can't breath," Nicholas gasped, pulling away from Gabriel. Taking up his glass again he drank and laughed and said, "Vacuum cleaner mouth, that's what you've got."

"The better to *suck* you with, my dear," Gabriel smirked and swallowed some wine.

They did order pizza. It was delivered, just before the movie came on, by an ancient Italian delivery boy. Nicholas tipped him five.

The pan pie was Chicago deep with various cheeses, sausage, pepperoni, garlic, spices-- in fact, the entire south-end of Taylor street was packed into that heavenly pie.

The wine, Chianti. "Well, what else?" Nicholas said as he opened the bottle. "We'll drink it all and make a candle holder for the bedroom. How's that for romantic, huh sugar?"

In the darkened room, light being there only by virtue of the turned on t.v. and a spying street lamp smiling quietly outside the windows, the Blue Danube Waltz played: a memorial musical monument to a memorable lingering movie scene-- the graceful turning of the space station, a bright white 2001 space donut shining out against the black velvet universe; if truth be told though, a pristine galactic vagina slowly revolving with infinite feminine patience, serenely spinning, the Blue Danube Waltz accompanying her silver celestial dance. She awaits penetration. Like Salome she receives her gift. But this cosmic ballet will never end. Not, at least, until Zarathustra speaks.

⇧

In bed that night they talk, the earthling and the angel. They talk of movies that they have seen, and of the movie that they have just finished watching, together. And of dreams.

225

Gabriel says, "I've never been quite clear about the monolith. I think it's supposed to be God. What do you think?"

Nicholas says, "I think God is dead, thank God." He laughs, then says, "Yes. God. Probably. Probably God."

Gabriel says, "I think it's all about death. And that there really is no death. That things just are: really just are. Time is an illusion, death is an illusion, everything is just *This*. And, this *This* is not easy to understand. Oh, well, whatever it means," and he laughs.

They look at each other. They are happy. They have, for the moment, come together in Gabriel's *Thisness*. Nothing else really matters.

Nicholas turns his head and blows out the candle that is flickering in the empty Chianti bottle on the nightstand by the bed. They turn to each other then.

Holding each other tightly, as if one might lose the other in the night, they fall asleep in whisperings of their new love.

🏛

Nicholas and Gabriel walk naked, hand in hand, on the almost blinding diamond white sand that elegantly frames the blue green sea. The water, like icy glass, is shiny and flat. High above them, in a cloudless, fluid, tangerine sky, the giant red sun looks like a steaming wrinkled apple. A copious pastel beam of light arcs splendidly over the earth.

The empty land, stretching out before the sea moves endlessly on, until the visual plane becomes lost in the juncture of the horizon where the orange sky meets the white earth.

It is the serendipity of a dream.

They walk slowly forward, shoulder to shoulder.

Far to the side of them, somewhere in the center of the sea, the great monolith ladened with a galaxy of white gemstones rises silently to the surface of the water. The jewels, like solar cells, catch and hold the fire of the sun, trapping it to itself.

As the sun is directly above them, continually, they cast no shadows as they walk.

Perfectly, an absolute audio vacuum prevails. When they speak, their words are not sounds, not words that can be heard, but rather, thoughts put forth upon the unified field of understanding.

There also is no wind, not that there is a deficiency of air; there simply is no unnecessary movement on the land-plane, other than their own.

Peacefully orbiting the earth, disregarding day and night, the moon sweeps the sky. Its colorless gray light swings full circle in quick rotations around the planet accosting the steaming immobile sun with its cold transient indifference.

Gabriel looks directly ahead as he walks. His eyes glow with the occasion of serenity and fulfillment. Upon his lips there is cast a gentle smile as though perfect simplicity is its source. His gait is dignified with the precise awareness of himself, in relationship to his other self, that holds his hand. For he is leading this other self into liberation and that, after all, is the purpose of his existence.

"I am afraid to die," Nicholas says, *"for I have sinned."*

"There is no death. This is what I came to tell you," Gabriel reveals sagaciously.

They look at each other briefly, holding the other in the depths of their eyes. Again, they gaze out over the white land-plane that eternally extends itself before them.

"Yes, truly there is no death," Gabriel pauses looking back into his other face.

They both stop walking and as they do the moon above them halts its flight.

"Death is an illusion. Nothing actually dies. The truth, Nicholas, is that there is simply This.

"Nicholas--" And Gabriel takes both of Nicholas's hands firmly into his own. Staring endlessly into Nicholas's eyes, he continues speaking without the slightest increment of doubt: *"I am the universe seeing what it is like to be Gabriel. And when I have seen enough, I will simply go back to being the universe. There is no sin. No fault. No death. Nobody is at fault for anything. The universe is just too big for that."*

Nicholas smiles. Closing his eyes, quietly still, he lets his other's words penetrate into the lightless regions of his mind.

After a time his eyes open brightly, and Gabriel sees that Nicholas understands. There is light in his eyes.

Both turn away from the other. Releasing hands they continue walking without words, side by side, toward the horizon existing beyond the infinite whiteness of the sand.

The capricious moon, again dancing in the sky, peevishly speeds past the stolid sun.

And floating motionlessly on the waveless water of the green-glass sea, the great monolith sparkles in magnificence. Shooting uncountable starry rays forth, throughout every dimension of time and space, as an infant galaxy about to be born, the universe trembles in loving anticipation.